DAMN COMPUTERS

Damn Computers

John B. Eichler

Copyright © 2023 John B. Eichler
All rights reserved.

No part of this publication may be reproduced, distributed, or transmitted in any form or by any means, including photocopying, recording, or other electronic or mechanical methods, without the prior written permission of the publisher, except in the case of brief quotations embodied in critical reviews and certain other noncommercial uses permitted by copyright law. For permission requests contact the publisher.

Damn Computers
by John B. Eichler

ISBN: 979-8-9885190-0-3 (Paperback)

First edition 2023.

Front cover image and book design by Author.

Published by

Briggs-Vaughan Publishing
P.O. Box 7447
Little Rock, Arkansas 72217 USA
www.Briggs-Vaughan-Publishing.com
info@Briggs-Vaughan-Publishing.com

Dedicated to

My loving wife
Pat
—our children—
Brad, Joan, and Julie
—our grandchildren—
Alex, Max, Ben, Grace, Caroline, and Reece

Summary

This book summarizes my work with computers starting more than 60 years ago. It is not meant to be strictly oriented toward those who work with programming computers, but rather for a general audience interested in the trials and tribulations of a computer geek back when the words "computer geek" were unknown. It covers working with computers from vacuum tube days to the current day.

Nowadays nearly everyone uses computers on an almost daily basis not realizing what working with computers used to be in the old days. Hopefully, because of my personal experience, you can read this book and get a feeling for what those old days were like. It is, in a way, a history book viewed through the eyes of a systems programmer.

Every attempt has been made to make the presented material non-technical and easily grasped by the average reader. Anyone interested in computers, and particularly computer history, should find the material interesting. The goal is not to make you a computer whiz, but hopefully the book will contain at least some new information you have not previously encountered. At least I sincerely hope so.

Included is an extensive index that cross-references most of material covered. Also included are a number of illustrations to clarify what is discussed.

Contents

Dedication page i
Summary iii
Table of Contents v
List of Figures ix
List of Tables xi
Foreword xiii
Preface xvi
Acknowlegements xxi

1 IIT/ARF/IITRI days   **1**
    1.1 The Illinois Institute of Technology 1
    1.2 The project at ARF 2
    1.3 My first computer 5
    1.4 The UNIVAC 1105 8
    1.5 UNIVAC mainframe logic modules 16
    1.6 Scientific versus commercial computers in that era 17
    1.7 The UNIVAC 1105's high speed memory 18
    1.8 The UNIVAC 1105's operating system 19
    1.9 Programming the UNIVAC 1105 21
    1.10 Computer programming 22
    1.11 Applications 24
    1.12 The IBM 7094 35
    1.13 A few extra comments on IITRI 37

2 Boise Cascade days   **39**
    2.1 My search for a new position 40
    2.2 Showing the 360 who was its new master 43
    2.3 The first weeks on the model 30 45

	2.4	The project at Boise	48
	2.5	Moving on to greener pastures	51
3	**Dixon Days:**		
	Software to Women's wear	**53**
	3.1	New retailer in town	55
	3.2	The good and the bad	56
	3.3	Computer activities in Dixon	56
	3.4	Back to seeking greener pastures	57
4	**Telemed Days**	**59**
	4.1	Hello Interdata	60
	4.2	A simplified explanation of ECG analysis	61
		4.2.1 How the heart works	61
		4.2.2 The ECG cart	62
		4.2.3 Transmission of the ECG signal	63
		4.2.4 The ECG computer receiver	65
		4.2.5 Analysis and sending back the report	66
	4.3	Off to Princeton, New Jersey	66
	4.4	Back to Hoffman Estates, Illinois	67
	4.5	Telemed's first MEPC customer	69
	4.6	The Interdata 7/32	72
	4.7	My management style	73
	4.8	Yearly cardiology conventions	75
	4.9	Further comments on computer multitasking	76
	4.10	Other reminiscences from Telemed	77
	4.11	Corporate politics	82
5	**Analysts International Days**	**87**
	5.1	The hospital in trouble	88
	5.2	United 'X' Corporation and COBOL	89
	5.3	Telemed as a client	90
6	**ECG Systems Days**	**93**
	6.1	Moving to Little Rock	94
	6.2	The IBM Bonner analysis program	94
	6.3	Introduction to hardware design	96
	6.4	My secret ingredient	99
	6.5	A few comments on core memory	100

6.6	Remote changes to our system	102
6.7	A weird trip to New Jersey	103
6.8	Trouble was lurking in the wings	104

7 Gunn Systems Days   105
    7.1 The carpet unroller 106

8 Dillards Days   111
    8.1 Bulletin boards and Usenet 111
    8.2 Getting a job through the BBS contact 112

9 Acxiom Days   115
    9.1 When a team is not a team 116
    9.2 Read the damn manual 117
    9.3 Toastmasters at Acxiom 117
    9.4 Seeking greener pastures once again 118

10 Calculator project   121
    10.1 Calculator design phase 122
    10.2 Programming the device 126
    10.3 The finished calculator 126

11 Election Resources Days   129
    11.1 My first project at ERC 130
    11.2 A sudden change in direction 131
    11.3 The data input program webpage 132
    11.4 Working with a perfectionist boss 133
    11.5 Election night results 135
    11.6 One nasty bug remained 135
    11.7 A "Big brother is watching you" program 136
    11.8 Ready to give up the ship 137

12 Retirement Days   139
    12.1 Back to school 140
    12.2 My Interdata Collection 142
    12.3 Other retirement activities 143
    12.4 Conclusion: Looking back 145

Appendices 147

A Bits, nybbles, bytes, words: A primer 149
- A.1 Possible combinations of 'n' bits 150
- A.2 Common number bases used 151
- A.3 Industry standardization 152
- A.4 Covering all my bases 153

B Simplified election reports 155
- B.1 Election contests and ballot design 155
- B.2 An example of a typical election 157
  - B.2.1 Summary reports 157
  - B.2.2 Contest reports 160
- B.3 Hyperlinking all the report webpages 160

C What is microprogramming 165
- C.1 The problem 165
- C.2 Computer timing 166

About this book 169

Index 171

List of Figures

1.1   1960 IIT and ARF physical layout.   2
1.2   Strong shock tube.   3
1.3   Strong shock tube (another view).   4
1.4   IBM 650 computer.   5
1.5   Vacuum tubes.   6
1.6   IBM 650 drum storage unit.   7
1.7   Overall view of the UNIVAC 1105.   9
1.8   ARF's UNIVAC 1105 configuration. 10
1.9   View of the UNIVAC 1105 controls. 11
1.10 UNIVAC 1105 operator console. 12
1.11 UNIVAC 1105 high speed offline printer. 14
1.12 UNIVAC 1105 high speed printer drum. 15
1.13 UNIVAC 1105 vacuum tube logic module. 16
1.14 UNIVAC 1105 core memory stack. 18
1.15 The SWIMM code final report to the AEC. 27
1.16 The "jerry-rigged" terminal for the UNIVAC 1105. 30
1.17 A Polaroid picture of the type that is displayed. 31
1.18 An Ampex commercial tape recorder. 32
1.19 IBM 7094 transistorized scientific mainframe computer. . 36

2.1   An IBM 360/model 30 computer system. 41
2.2   An IBM 1311 hard disk storage unit. 42
2.3   An IBM 360/model 30 system console. 46

3.1   The front of our 3-floor store in Dixon. 54
3.2   A small portion of the first floor of our store in Dixon. . . 55

4.1   An electrocardiogram (ECG) cart. 63

4.2	Typical components for an ECG analysis system.	65
4.3	An electrocardiogram (ECG) cart.	70
4.4	The MEPC electrocardiogram (ECG) processing system.	71
4.5	The EPIC ECG processing system.	73
4.6	10 MB Pertec hard disk drive.	78
4.7	300 MB CDC disk pack.	78
6.1	The ECG Systems "Med-Call" unit.	98
6.2	Core memory details.	101
6.3	Interdata 64KB memory circuit board.	101
7.1	Rotary shaft encoder.	107
7.2	LED six digit display.	108
10.1	The Motorola microcomputer overview schematic.	123
10.2	Calculator circuit board details.	124
10.3	The calculator test rig.	125
10.4	The final finished calculator.	127
12.1	The Interdata console.	142
12.2	One of my old Interdata 7/32 machines.	144
12.3	Interdata console.	144
12.4	Interdata display terminal.	144
B.1	Report voting levels.	158
B.2	Voting summary reports.	159
B.3	County contest reports.	160
B.4	Precinct contest reports.	161
B.5	Hyperlinking of result reports.	163
C.1	Microprogramming level diagram.	168

List of Tables

A.1 Number of combinations 2^n possible for 'n' bits 150
A.2 Counting in different base number systems 152

Foreword

John and I first crossed paths over 25 years ago when we both worked as developers for Acxiom. Unfortunately, little came of that meeting because we worked in entirely different departments. We fully connected several years later as a result of our wives volunteering at a library in Little Rock. They had an invitation to the library Christmas party, and the four of us sat together. John and I, realizing we had worked together at Acxiom many years before, struck up a conversation. He and I have been friends ever since.

One of the many reasons that John and I relate on a personal level is the similarity of our professional background. While I followed a more traditional corporate route than he did, we were both there when the use of computers in science and industry really began to take off. I went to work for IBM and was quickly sent to Basic Computer Training, a three month crash course in the theory and operation of digital computers. After a year of on the job training I went back for another three month course, this one entitled Basic Systems Training. We learned operating systems, systems programming, file design, telecommunications, and programming, from System/360 assembler to COBOL (which I disliked as much as John did.) Upon completion of the class I was assigned a brand new IBM system, the 1130, which had been designed as an engineering solution. IBM salesmen saw it as a low-cost entry for commercial applications and sold a lot of them. The fact that there were no commercial applications available or that the only programming language available was FORTRAN (designed for scientists and engineers) were not seen as problems.

I was called on to design and program complete systems, such as order entry, billing, inventory control, payroll, and all manner of reports. Along the way I created my own systems for indexed files, sorts, backup, and file maintenance. For the first few years all this was complicated by the fact that the 1130 had a single removable hard drive (a whopping one megabyte, by the way). One of the most innovative applications I created was one to add, delete, and change records in a sequential file that consumed most of the hard drive. It would be trivial with two drives, not so much with only one. And one more thing: The 1130 came with, at most, 8K (8,192 to be precise) 16-bit words, approximately equal to 16K bytes. I learned to use every bit.

Later in my career I was fortunate to be selected to attend what amounted to IBM graduate school at their Systems Research Institute in New York City. We were given access to and trained by experts in hardware design, operating systems, and telecommunications. After returning to the office I undertook more complex systems, such as implementing a complete nursing station system for a large hospital (which required writing a video display emulator) and adding video capability to a process control machine. Neither of those systems had been attempted within IBM before. Creating the terminal emulator later earned me a six-week assignment in Germany, assisting a large customer with a similar problem.

Readers will likely surmise John's native intelligence while progressing through the book, but he often writes as though his experiences were commonplace. They were not. As one who has been down the same path, I can assure you that John is being disarmingly modest when he casually says I bought the book, read about the system, and began programming it. Computer manuals, especially in the early days, were written as reference books, not tutorials. The authors assumed that you knew what you were doing and just needed a refresher. The books would give a technical description of, say, a computer instruction, with no hint as to why or where you might use it in a program. That part was up to you. After the design and coding phase, every system had a different and sometimes maddening program translation process. This process was intended to take your program from the written source code to an executable program. Heaven help you if your program did run but failed in execution. Supplied debugging aids were few. As John describes, a program failure often reduced the programmer to reading core dumps in octal or hexadecimal to determine the cause. Reading core dumps, watching the pattern of the console lights, or simply listening to the noises the computer made (yes, they did) were finely tuned skills of experienced programmers.

In addition, hidden dangers would lurk for those brave enough to delve into or interface with operating system routines, which John did on a regular basis. I find it remarkable that he gained all the necessary expertise on his own, which would have required a significant number of hours of concentrated effort. Sometimes when things didn't work right, you just kept working on them till they did. It was said of our profession that any of us who had not seen the sun rise over a cpu— the computer's central processing unit—couldn't truly be considered a programmer. Given John's experiences, I suspect that he saw many sunrises in that manner. Along the way he simply invented ingenious solutions to the problems he encountered. And finally, in my experience it is highly unusual for someone to be equally adept at all three levels of development: application programming, systems programming, and hardware design and implementation. Most people are content to focus on one and call for help if in trouble with either of the others. Except, of course, for John.

As authentic dinosaurs, veterans of the early days of the computer revolution, John and I have traded many war stories. Through the years I gained some insights into John's personal and technical history, but this book filled in many gaps and added new experiences. At one level, John's story is a history of nearly sixty years of computing, beginning with vacuum tubes, core memory, and hand-soldered components. You can follow advances in the science of computers, both hardware and software, from the beginning of his career to the end. And then, on another level, you can come to understand John's work history, which is varied and wide-ranging. Both perspectives, in my view, are informing and fascinating.

Just like "Star Trek," John's story is an ongoing mission. The book briefly discusses his life after retirement: continuing education, creative writing, and his long-term interest in geoscience. He doesn't talk about his filmmaking or his love of opera or the other two or three things on his mind today. It is an understatement to say that he is an interesting and interested person, and I hope you enjoy his memoir as much as I did.

Ron Eddy
Little Rock, AR
November, 2022

Preface

Historically each generation has new technology thrust upon it. My grandfather witnessed the blossoming of the industrial revolution. My father—born just before the turn of the last century—saw the rise of mass production with the coming of the automobile and the airplane, not to mention both world wars. And now my generation, which, in my opinion, has been the most exciting generation of them all.

I was born just prior to World War II, which saw the development of reasonably modern, yet rudimentary, electronic instrumentation including radar, early computers, sophisticated rocketry and the atomic bomb. The next ten-year period following the war experienced an exponential growth eclipsing all that came before. The most significant advancement—at least to me—was the development of the transistor by Bell Labs in the mid 1940s.

In 1957, my first year in college at the Illinois Institute of Technology in Chicago, the first artificial satellite was launched into orbit. I quickly developed an interest in rockets that became almost an obsession during my first two years at school. IIT had no rocket society on campus so a few of my fellow students started one at my urging.

But IIT did have an on-campus research arm called the Armour Research Foundation (ARF) whose name was later changed to the Illinois Institute of Technology Research Institute (IITRI). ARF engaged in both government and industrial research activities. Best of all, they had a number of scientists who were engaged in rocket research. Upon learning this, I immediately invited a few of them to attend our rocket society meetings and talk to the members. Two of these scientists became friends of mine. One was Paul Lieberman who worked on rockets in the military and was, at that time, working on his PhD. The other was Chuck Meese, a mathematician who was an expert on fuel droplets as the fuel entered rocket engines. Both of these men, especially Paul, were good contacts to have as it later turned out.

Paul was heavily involved in a research project for the Atomic Energy Commission, a government agency which regulates safety aspects of nuclear reactors. They were worried about a reactor malfunction such as what happened much later at Chernobyl. The AEC commissioned ARF to do an extensive study of reactor containment involving numerous experimental and theoretical areas.

In 1959 Paul had some serious data reduction requirements that were carried out using large mechanical calculators with more keys than one can imagine. These machines were nothing more than adding machines with the additional capabilities of doing both multiplication and division. Paul asked if I might be interested in working part time cranking out numbers for him. I jumped at the chance. Getting my foot in the door at ARF was a golden opportunity for me.

I worked that summer and when fall came, I asked Paul if I might work full-time while I finished my degree in evening school. He said that would be fine, and he seemed happy to have me onboard. Hence my 8 years stint at ARF/IITRI began.

I had a double major of math and physics at school and, like most mathematicians, I was somewhat lazy and the continual pounding out calculations on an adding machine seemed to me to be boring at best. I heard that the institute had a "high speed" computer in the physics building, and I wanted to see what a real computer looked like firsthand. The only time I had seen one before was on television cranking out election results. Little did I know then that computers and I would become friends—and foes—for the next six decades.

Unlike many in the computer field today, I became curious as to how computers really worked on a fundamental basis. This curiosity led to not only computer software, but eventually to hardware as well.

Books on computers—at least to a causal observers—tend to seem overly technical but I've attempted to make this book completely readable by almost all audiences.

Einstein once said, when asked about his Theory of Relativity, that one didn't understand a topic well if they were not able to explain it to his or her grandmother. I have strived to make this book understandable to my grandmother. At this stage in my life, I know a lot of grandmothers—my wife being one of them—that I've had read this material and, amazingly, they understand it. Now at times, in order to explain a topic, I will present some technical background but only to the depth required and not in a technical way. This book is not designed as a technical one but rather one that relates my experiences having grown up during the relatively early days of computers. This is a first hand account of what it was like romping in computerland for all these years.

Enjoy!

John B. Eichler
Little Rock, AR

Acknowledgements

In writing a book like this I owe a debt of gratitude to all the people who have given me the latitude to pursue my deep-seated interest in computer technology. Without their patience and encouragement this book would have not been possible in the first place.

In particular I'd first like to express my heartfelt thanks to my wife, Pat, and our children: Brad, Joan, and Julie. They were without my presence due to late nights and weekends spent fighting computer bugs. I was sure that being gone so much was a real burden on family life. Over the years I have heard them each individually express the desire to never touch a computer as long as they lived. Happily they all now work daily with computers for work and pleasure.

For this book, as well as other writings I have done over the years, my first editor, encourager, motivator, and supporter has always been my wife Pat. She has always been my guinea pig as to whether or not what I have written will fly or land like a lead balloon. Her keen eye for all my blunders, misspellings, and wrong phraseology has been invaluable to me.

I have two friends to whom I'd also like to express my deep gratitude for many hours they spent reading, rereading, and then rereading again this book to give me feedback. The first is Ron Eddy who has graciously had the fortitude to proofread many of my writings and has made valuable suggestions that have greatly improved the readability of my scribblings so they convey the meaning I intended. Ron's vast knowledge of computers has kept me on the straight and narrow. He also deserves my heartfelt thanks for writing a foreword for this book.

The second friend who has proven valuable in the creation of this book is James Robert (Bob) Ward. I don't know how Bob does it but his keen eye for errors all the rest of us have missed, over multiple readings, is nothing short of amazing. Just as we think we have found all the possible errors, Bob would find something else that must be corrected.

I also want to express my appreciation to my cousin, Carol Iskowich, to whom I gave the book to read not realizing she had been an English major in college. What I got back was the book with grammatical errors highlighted on numerous pages. My thanks goes to Carol for her unexpected, but much appreciated, contribution to this book.

I must furthermore extend my thanks to our daughter, Professor Joan Simon. I gave the book to her for any final comments and got back so many helpful comments and suggestions it reminded me of how my college writing instructors used to grade my papers. It looked like a chicken with ink on it's feet walked over every page. Having someone so close, so accomplished, and so proficient in proofreading theses and dissertations over many years is a benefit I'd bet many other writer's would be envious of. Thanks Joan.

When finally I thought I had, with the help of all those mentioned above, ferreted every last error in the book, I gave the manuscript to my daughter's mother-in-law, Donna Simon, since she expressed interest in reading the fruits of my labor. To my amazement she read the book and produced for me an addditional list of previously undetected corrections. When I quizzed her about her proofreading skills, she told me she had worked for seven years editing the writings of a Pulitzer Prize winning newspaper man. What a surprise! Thanks Donna.

Without such a loyal family and friends this book would not exist.

1
IIT/ARF/IITRI days

1.1 The Illinois Institute of Technology

In the summer of 1959, after attending college at the Illinois Institute of Technology in Chicago for two years, I started working part time at the Illinois Institute of Technology Research Institute (IITRI)—then called the Armour Research Foundation (ARF). When fall of that year rolled around, I had the opportunity to work full time and decided to finish my degree in evening school even though it would take me an extra year. The building I worked in was at the northwest corner of the intersection of 34th and Dearborn in an old building that was a hangover from a temporary building (number 17) from the World War 2 era. (A map of the IIT campus is shown in Figure 1.1.) We affectionately referred to the building as a permanent/temporary building—resembling an military barracks—being a single story structure to be later torn down.

Across the street on the southwest corner was a very old typical brick school building (not shown on the map) that was no longer being used. Next to it on the south was a two story new building (number 16) housing some of the research institute's staff. That building was extended, after the school was torn down, into the building as now shown on the map.

On the northeast corner of the intersections was one of IIT's most interesting buildings on campus: Crown Hall (number 26) that housed the IIT School of Architecture. During my junior year at the school I attended a prom there where the band leader was none other than Duke Ellington.

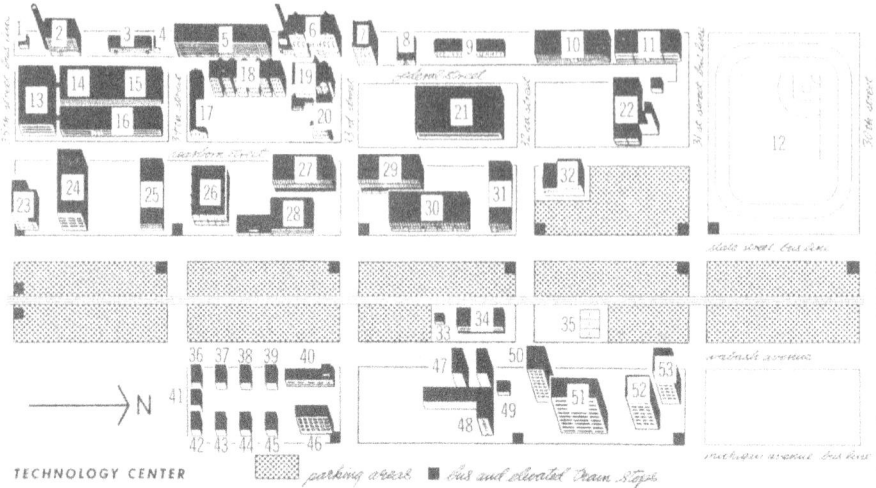

Figure 1.1: 1960 IIT and ARF physical layout. (SOURCE: 1960 IIT campus phone book.)

1.2 The project at ARF

The U.S. Atomic Energy Commission (AEC), fearing a reactor meltdown accident, had given a large government contract to ARF to conduct a safety study on nuclear reactors. Of primary concern was reactor overheating—just like what occurred in 1986 at Chernobyl—resulting in a violent chemical, not nuclear, explosion. Since a high pressure liquid was used to transfer heat from the reactor core, the liquid would explosively decompress causing a violent explosion. The whole idea was to develop a blast-shield to contain the explosion so that radioactive material would not be released to the area around the reactor thus producing high levels of radioactivity contamination.

To study the effects of such an explosion we experimentally produced a contained explosion in a device called a strong shock tube. Our shock tube was nothing more than an eighteen foot steel tube made up of a series of three foot sections with the tube portion being a four inch diameter steel tube having one inch thick walls to contain the controlled explosion. This tube was divided into two parts: a six foot upper high pressure section and a twelve foot lower pressure section with the sections separated by either a plastic or metal diaphragm. We would pressurize

1.2 The project at ARF

the high pressure section until the diaphragm ruptured sending a high pressure shock wave—emulating an explosion—down the lower pressure section and hence the name shock tube (see Figure 1.2).

Figure 1.2: Strong shock tube. (SOURCE: From one of the reports we made to the AEC.)

At the end of the low pressure system we would build a test shield structure out of materials such as wood that were two inches in diameter to see how it crushed under explosive shock wave loading. Of course this could prove dangerous so we built a blast shield to protect us when conducting experiments. This was nothing more than two four-foot by eight-foot pieces of three-quarter inch plywood separated by six inches of sand. To see out from behind the shield, we installed a four inch thick piece of bulletproof glass at a viewable height.

To instrument the experiment we used high speed oscilloscopes—an electronic device—to record how the pressure rose over a very brief time measured in milliseconds, i.e., one thousandth of a second. The outputs were Polaroid pictures, the same as a regular Polaroid camera would produce (cameras are shown on two of the oscilloscopes). The only difference was with these pictures the oscilloscope would superimpose a grid enabling us make relatively precise measurements of pressure as the shock wave hit the sample under test (see Figure 1.17). My job was to carefully measure the height of the wave at different intervals to see how sample crushing was occurring. As one may guess, it was a boring job involving my use of a calculator to adjust all the pressure levels to a calibrated level. Because my job involved experimental data, I found myself spending more and more time in the actual laboratory.

Figure 1.3: Strong shock tube (a view showing Ed Murry on left operating one of the oscilloscopes and Paul Lieberman, my boss, operating the controls). (SOURCE: From one of the reports we made to the AEC.)

I heard that the research institute had an electronic computer, and I anxiously wanted to see it. It was located in the physics building across the street (building number 24 in Figure 1.1). I finally got my wish granted.

1.3 My first computer

In late 1959 computers were still somewhat of a rarity. ARF had an old IBM 650 computer, a machine introduced around 1953 that was based on vacuum tube technology.

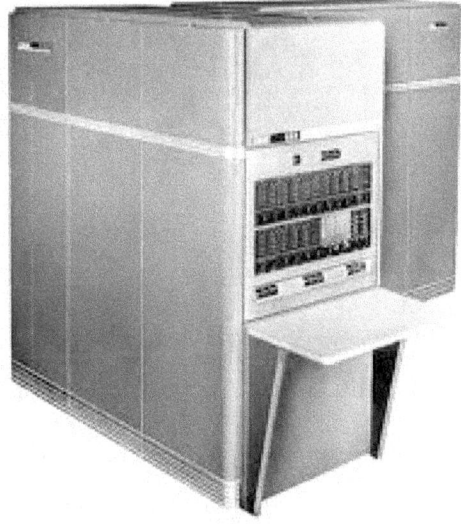

Figure 1.4: IBM 650 computer. (SOURCE: Original source unknown but believed to be IBM.)

All computers are basically devices that use high speed switches configured to do logic operations. These switches are just like common light switches but had to open and close more rapidly. The very first computers in the early 1940s used relays to accomplish this function, but relays were slow. In the late 1940s the use of vacuum tubes, small glass tubes like the ones used in early radios that could, in a vacuum, provide the same switching functions but at much faster speeds (see Figures 1.5 and 1.13). Just think of a switch that would switch electrical currents on or off at a higher rate of speed. Today transistors provide the same function, but when the IBM 650 came out reliable transistors were not yet available on the commercial market.

It is interesting to note here that new technologies—like the transistor that was invented in 1947—usually take a number of years to come into widespread commercial use. That being the case, in the 1950s most computers, especially the large ones, were designed using vacuum tubes. Since vacuum tubes were power hungry, large machines required serious air conditioning. The IBM 650 was small enough that no large air conditioner was needed but rather used fans to keep the components cool enough to operate.

Figure 1.5: Vacuum tubes. (SOURCE: Original source unknown.)

It is useful at this point to give some idea of the timing of computer operations. Relays took tenths of a second to turn currents on or off. Vacuum tubes cut this time down to milliseconds—one thousandths of a second—or less and hence were a thousand times faster than using relays. Transistors, on the other hand, have switching times in microseconds—one millionth of a second—or less being a thousand times faster than vacuum tubes. Today transistor switching times are measured in nanoseconds—one billionth of a second—or less. But we are getting ahead of ourselves here.

I was fascinated by the IBM 650. Because computers were a new technology, there were no computer classes in any except a few institutions. Computer science wasn't mentioned in course catalogues, and few people I worked with knew much about them. At ARF there was a computer group comprised mainly of mathematicians but in the hydrodynamics area I was working in, only a few brave souls used them. Those that did were considered a rare breed.

I immediately bought a manual on the IBM 650 and started studying

1.3 My first computer

the beast. The 650 was an interesting machine and was nothing more than a programmable calculator. The architecture[1] of computers can be varied, to some extent, to increase the performance of the machine. The 650 was quite different than most later machines. At the time the 650 was designed, disk storage had not been invented and neither had high speed random access memory (RAM). Hence the arithmetic section consisted basically of an accumulator that was divided into an upper and lower register in which numbers could be loaded and an operation such as add or subtract could be done.

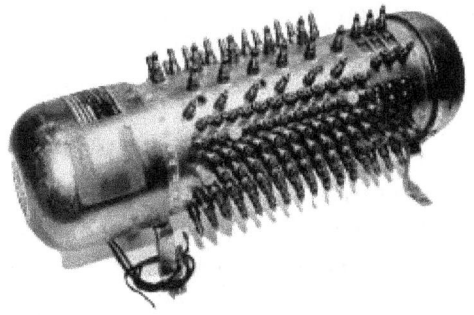

Figure 1.6: IBM drum storage unit. (SOURCE: Original source unknown but probably IBM.)

Since there was no high speed RAM memory on the machine, a "drum" unit was added. This drum was nothing more than a cylinder ro-

---

[1] The same way the architecture of a house refers to the design of the house, the architecture of a computer refers to how the computer was designed. Depending on the skill of the designer, the resultant computer can be oriented, to some extent, toward the purpose for which the machine is to be used. This being said, most computers are designed as general purpose machines to make them as versatile as possible in a wide range of applications. Such machines generally contain a number of separate components like memory—both high speed, like random access memory (RAM) and slow speed like a drum or disk—where both the program and data are stored as well as data. Another component is the control circuitry that executes the program logic. Still another is the computational circuitry that does the arithmetic and logic testing. The classic architecture is typically called "von Neumann" after a design created by mathematician John von Neumann in the 1940s. A principle feature of this architecture is that the high speed memory may hold both the program being executed as well as the data being worked on to make operations very fast. More on this later.

tating at a high speed and having a number of read/write heads—similar to a tape recorder's read/write heads. The result was a matrix of sorts that could be represented on paper into a series of rows and columns. In all, there were a total of 2,000 locations where either a program or data could be stored. Since the drum was rotating continuously, once one location had been either read from or written to, one had to wait until the drum completed one complete rotation before that location could be read from or written to again. Because the rotational speed was known, a clever programmer could arrange both the instructions and the data in a manner such that the next location needed—for either program or data—would be under one of the read/write heads next. Thus, unlike computers today, the placement of locations could be strategically placed to greatly decrease the running time of whatever program was running. Such a method is no longer required for all modern computers.

Each location containing an instruction—such as load, store, add, subtract, test, etc.—was formatted as a 10-digit number. The first 2 digits specified the operation required. These 2-digits are referred to as the operation code (op-code for short). The circuitry decodes each op-code and performs the required operation[2]. The op-code concept has essentially filtered down today to nearly all computers. The next 4-digits represented the data location required by the instruction, i.e., 0 through 1,999, and the last 4-digits the location of the next instruction to be executed.

Once I finished studying the IBM 650, I was ready to write my first program. Unfortunately before I got an opportunity to write a program for this machine, it was hauled out of ARF and replaced by a new massive machine, the UNIVAC 1105.

1.4 The UNIVAC 1105

The UNIVAC 1105 was an upgrade to the earlier UNIVAC machines—the 1103 and the 1103A—and retained their general architecture. At the time it was the largest vacuum tube machine UNIVAC made, cost over

---

[2]It is interesting to note that the basic instruction repertoire of most computers are very similar. Therefore, it's quite easy for someone to migrate from one machine to another. Later machines have added new more powerful instructions but these usually provide some specialized functionality and could be done with software instead using the basic instruction set.

1.4 The UNIVAC 1105

$2,000,000, and rented for around $25,000 a month. An overall view of the UNIVAC 1105 is shown in Figure 1.7. ARF had a contract with the U.S. Census Bureau that justified the acquisition of the machine. At night the 1105 was used by census bureau personnel to help with the analysis of the 1960 census and then it was available for use by ARF personnel during the day. Interestingly, it seemed that the machine was down for maintenance perhaps 40 percent of the time.

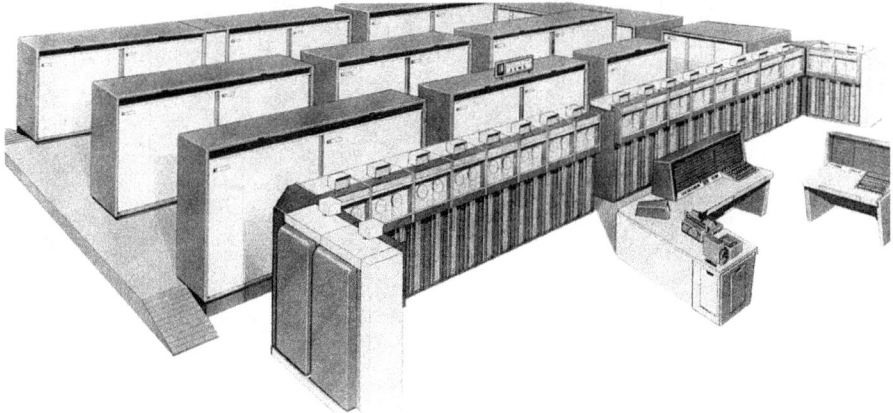

Figure 1.7: Overall view of the UNIVAC 105. (SOURCE: Original source unknown but likely Sperry Rand Corporation.)

There were, to the best of my knowledge, only seven of these machines built with three used by the Air Force, two at the University of North Carolina (also used for the census), the one at ARF, and one at the Prudential Insurance Company. The machine was a vacuum tube machine and used power like it was going out of style.

ARF hired a staff of operators that ran the various applications using the machine. Over the years I used the machine I became so familiar with the 1105 that when I was running programs on it, the operators would let me operate the monster as they would take a cigarette break. Naturally such a large investment in the system, my projects would be billed at the rate of $650 per hour. Incidentally, that was far more than I was making per month back then. Fortunately, the AEC had deep pockets so this was not a major problem. Each year when I wrote a proposal for work continuation, I would just add in the estimated amount I needed for my project.

Figure 1.8: ARF's UNIVAC 105 configuration. (SOURCE: Original source unknown but likely from ARF.)(Note: I am the 3rd person from the left partially hidden.)

The 1105 computer required a room 50 foot by 65 foot and a 30 ton air conditioner. That is the size of a 3,250 square foot house! It consisted of several rows of electronic cabinets on a raised floor such that each cabinet could be cooled. This air conditioning was supported by a water cooled unit. The water was provided by the city of Chicago where the water was taken from Lake Michigan. This water was not the cleanest because the pumps used would take in a number of fish and other impurities. I remember one time when the filters on the air conditioner were clogged by this debris and this took the computer down. This incident made the front page of some of Chicago's newspapers.

Since I spent many years on and off using this machine, I'm going to go into some detail in my description of this machine for a couple reasons. First, it was an early machine that I came to intimately know inside out. Second, the architecture of the 1105—both from a hardware and software perspective—was significantly different than that of computers as we know them today. A closer view of the control console is shown in Figure 1.9.

1.4 The UNIVAC 1105

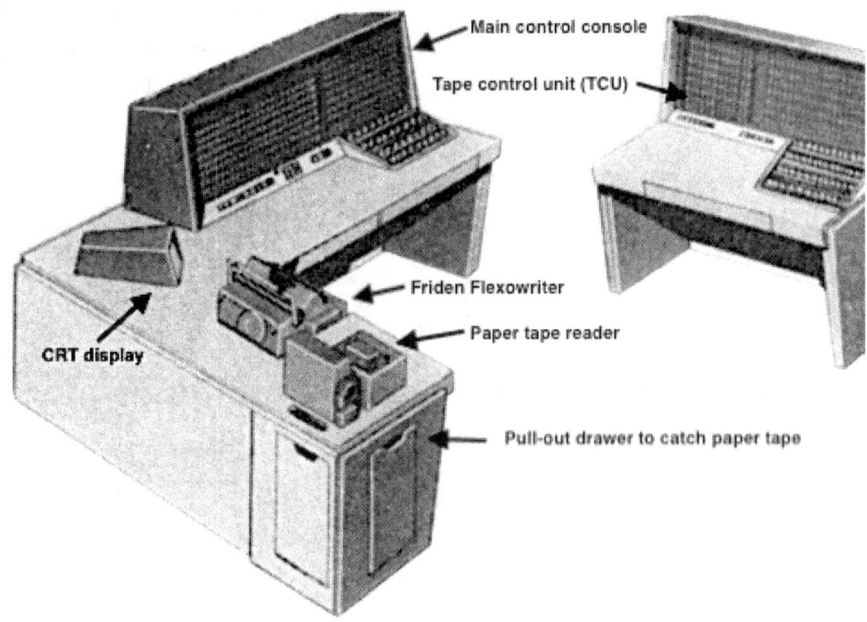

Figure 1.9: View of the UNIVAC 1105 operator controls. (SOURCE: Original source unknown but likely Sperry Rand Corporation modified with captions I put in.)

The operator's console consisted of several components. First, the input to the machine from the a programmer's point of view was a paper tape reader that read input at an amazingly fast 10 characters per second. I have seen some references that state the input speed as 200 characters per second so it could have been that fast. The paper tape was 1 inch wide with each row—in the short dimension—containing one character. There was a drawer that could be pulled out to catch the paper tape as it came out of the reader. I wished that it read IBM cards but that was an expensive option that ARF did not feel a necessity. When creating a paper tape using an old teletype machine, the paper tape could become quite long. I usually wound the paper tape so it resembled a roll of toilet paper being 1 inch wide and perhaps 4 to 6 inches in diameter. Every so often I would accidentally drop a roll and it was a real pain getting it rewound. Luckily, since the computer stored my programs on magnetic tape, corrections only involved repunching the program lines needing to be changed.

Next to the reader was a Friden Flexowriter, essentially a typewriter with a paper tape punch. This unit was seldom used by the computer itself unlike later machines that extensively used a typewriter-type device to communicate with the operating system. In fact, the 1105 lacked an operating system (to be explained later) like modern machines have.

Figure 1.10: UNIVAC 1105 operator console (SOURCE: Original source unknown but likely ARF.)

The main control panel had a zillion lights and buttons that flashed like mad as the machine was running a program. Figure 1.10 shows a better closeup of the operator console. Most programmers did not venture toward the console having the operators perform the function of actual machine operation. As I became more familiar with the 1105, I eventually was able to operate the console as well as any of the operators.

The tape drives were divided into 2 banks of 9 drives each and were controlled by a tape control unit (TCU). One tape bank was to the left of the operator's console, while the other bank was to the right. Each bank had a separate control unit capable of temporarily storing 120 computer words, roughly equivalent to 540 bytes of storage. The purpose of this storage was so the computer could read or write a block of storage at high

1.4 The UNIVAC 1105

speed freeing the computer to continue to run a program while the TCU would read or write to a magnetic tape. Having two control units was very useful as I found out later when I bet one of the senior programmers $5 I could do a particular operation, and he lost (and never paid up!).

One of the unique features of the 1105 was the cathode ray tube CRT display—similar to an early televison display—that deserves some explanation. I have never seen any such device on any other computer after the 1105. The machine had 8,192 words of high speed memory. Note that the byte had not yet been invented! This memory was divided into 2 banks of 4,096 words. It turns out that 4,096 is just 64 times 64, a fact that the machine designers used with this display. Imagine a square having 64 rows and 64 columns (4,096 distinctive points). Every time a high speed memory location was accessed, a bright dot would appear at one of these points. Since there were 2 memory banks, one didn't know which memory bank is being accessed, which was a minor inconvenience.

The nice thing about having this information displayed was that if you knew how your program was accessing memory, patterns would emerge that became familiar to the programmer. Sometimes when programming, a condition arises where unintentionally an "infinite loop" loop is created. The program will keep executing this loop over and over for the rest of time (or the computer is manually stopped). The result is that a recognizable pattern of dots is shown which indicates that something is wrong with the program, a very, very handy feature indeed.

Figure 1.11 shows a high speed printer that printed at the speed of 500 lines per minute. It was considered inefficient to have the 1105 directly control the printing from the mainframe itself. Hence all printed output from a program was directed to a magnetic tape that was removed and taken to a separate room having the printer and a tape drive to read the printed output and do the actual printing.

This printing substation had two rather large cabinets containing the circuitry to drive the printer. Like all equipment in those days, glitches were more the norm rather than exception. The printer, like the computer itself, was down for maintenance a large percentage of the time. Also, unlike with the computer's cabinets, the printer electronics cabinets were not air conditioned lending itself to heat build up.

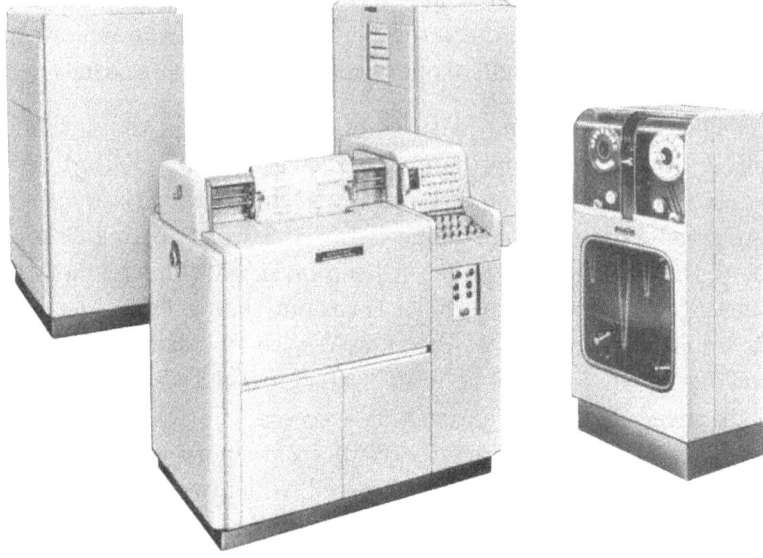

Figure 1.11: UNIVAC 1105 high speed offline printer. (SOURCE: Original source was a Sperry Rand Corporation sales brochure.)

Each cabinet contained a hinged door on either end of the long dimension of the cabinet. When it was summer and the building's air conditioner was having a hard time keeping the building cool, we would open both of the cabinet's doors and place regular big house fans on either end to provide a breeze to keep the vacuum tubes cool. A really low tech solution to a high tech problem. Definitely make-shift, but it worked like a charm.

Most early large-scale scientific mainframes had external printers because printing, especially if there was a printer problem, would really slow down the computer where time was expensive. In later days when more sophisticated operating systems were introduced having capability to do multitasking, i.e., run multiple tasks concurrently, this was less of a problem and printers were connected directly to the computer. With the 1105's printer, the tapes would frequently not be read correctly and it was the job of one of the operators to manipulate rereading the tape to get the printing completed.

1.4 The UNIVAC 1105

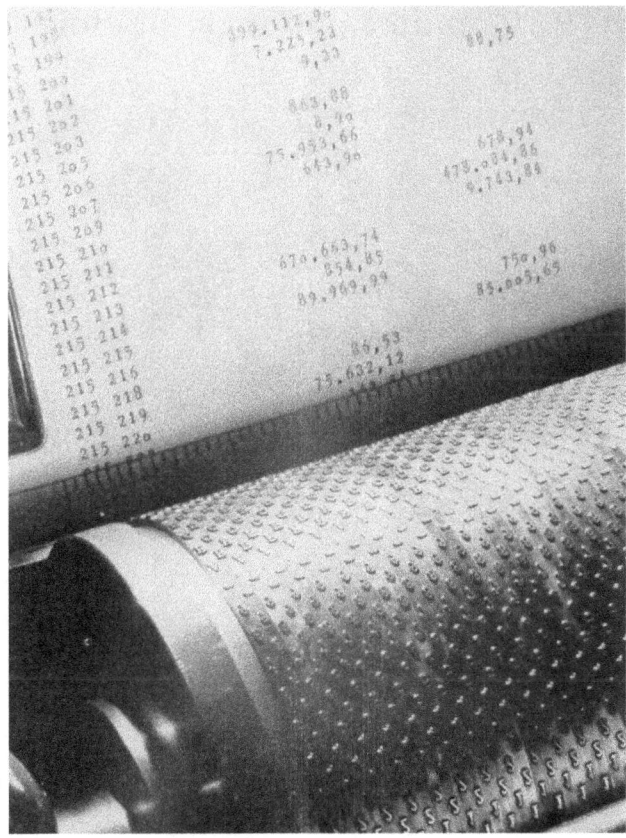

Figure 1.12: UNIVAC 1105 high speed printer drum. (SOURCE: Original source unknown but was likely the Sperry Rand Corporation.)

The operation of the printer was quite interesting also. On the side of the paper to be printed on there was a cylinder as shown in Figure 1.12 that contained all the characters that could be printed in circular patterns for each column to be printed. This cylinder rotated at a high speed and when a particular character in a particular column had to be printed, a hammer from behind the printer would come forward pushing the paper toward the drum. A ribbon would be situated between this cylinder and the paper. This meant that to print one line on the paper the drum would have to rotate many times to print all the characters on the line before the paper could be advanced. In later years, high speed printers used a rapidly rotating horizontal belt containing a single line of all the characters that could be printed.

1.5 UNIVAC mainframe logic modules

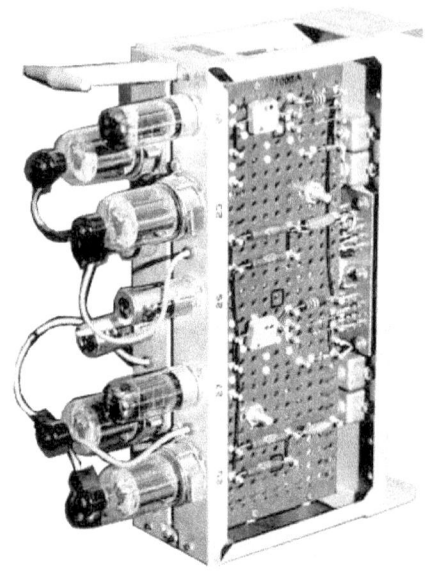

Figure 1.13: UNIVAC 1105 vacuum tube logic module. (SOURCE: Original source unknown but likely Sperry Rand Corporation.)

The 1105 electronics cabinets each contained an array of logic modules. A typical vacuum tube logic module for the 1105 is shown in Figure 1.13. These modules were accessible through sliding doors on the long side of each cabinet. Behind the logic modules was an extensive network of wiring connecting the modules to each other. When a problem occurred, it was seldom that the interconnecting wiring was the problem. It was usually a module went wrong—perhaps a vacuum tube burned out, etc.—so the entire module could be yanked out and replaced with a workable module. The bad module was given to an engineer—there were several full time engineers required to maintain the system—who would analyze the problem and repair the module. It is notable that today the logic for one module would be smaller than the sharp end of a pin on a modern integrated circuit.

1.6 Scientific versus commercial computers in that era

The basic element of storage in a computer is a single *bit*. A bit is nothing more that a switch that is either off or on. In computers the representation of a bit is either a 0 (zero) for off and a 1 (one) for on. This is referred to as a binary condition, i.e., only two states may occur. A single bit then can only represent one state or *binary digit*, i.e., 0 or 1. As such, a single bit is not very useful by itself.[3]

To make some unit of storage useful, a series of bits are grouped together so some information may be stored by the group. The most common basic grouping on today's machines is the *byte* which contains 8 binary switches. But when the 1105 came out, as mentioned earlier, the byte had not yet been invented. Hence, early computers grouped bits together in all kinds of weird bit groupings. There were 5-bit machines, 7-bit machines, 12-bit machines, etc.—in short there was a hodgepodge of different machines each usually directed toward specific end user applications.

Scientific oriented machines needed to operate on large numbers required for scientific calculations whereas commercial machines tended to be character or digit oriented. The UNIVAC 1105 had a word length of 36-bits meaning that a single word could contain very large numbers. For very technical applications, two words could be combined together to make the number size quite astronomical.

By a similar technique used in Table A.1 on page 150, the same 2^n could be extended to show the maximum number sizes possible with different word lengths. With an 8-bit word, the maximum value that could be held is 255 (equal to 2^8 - 1)[4]. With a 16-bit word, the maximum number value would be 65,535 (equal to 2^{16} - 1) and for a 32-bit word length the maximum value would be 4,294,967,295 (equal to 2^{32} - 1).

The 1105 also had drum storage similar to the IBM 650's drum as shown in Figure 1.6. Whereas the 650 only could store 2,000 words, the 1105 drum could store 2^{15} words which amounted to 32,768 word locations. This storage was logically divided in half with each half being

---

[3]If you are not familiar with how computers store information using bits and bytes, please read Appendix A on page 149. It explains in simple understandable language all you need to know about this topic.

[4]Zero is counted as a number which is why one must be subtracted from the value.

referred to as drum A and drum B. Programmers could reference only drum A while drum B was used by the system. More on this later.

1.7 The UNIVAC 1105's high speed memory

Early computers had very limited high speed storage. Unlike the IBM 650—that had only two primary registers and no high speed memory—the 1105 had 8,192 words of *core memory*. Solid-state random access memory would only come about a decade or so later in the mid 1970s.

Figure 1.14: UNIVAC 105 core memory stack holding 4,096 36-bit words.
(SOURCE: Original source unknown but likely Sperry Rand Corporation.)

Core memory consisted of very small—but easily viewable—small donut-shaped rings of a material that could be magnetized in either of two polarities. A matrix of wires were passed through each core element and by directing the electric current in these wires each individual core could store on bit as a 0 or 1. A memory stack containing 4,096 words is shown in Figure 1.14. To obtain a total of 8,192 words two such stacks were required. And core memory was very, very expensive. (See section 6.5 on page 100 for additional comments on core memory.)

Each "layer" contained 4,096 tiny magnetic cores in a 64 by 64 matrix. By stacking 36 layers—as shown in the figure—each vertical line of cores would store one word of either data or a computer instruction. One particularly useful feature of core memory is that once a bit is flipped to either a 0 or 1, it is retained even if the power is removed. Years later I used this feature to retain the core's data to build a system where it was critical to get the computer up and running fast after power failures. For realtime systems this proved quite useful but I'm getting ahead of myself now. The cores themselves were very reliable but sometimes the electronics driving them would have failures.

The whole idea with high speed memory is that data can be read or written from either the drum or tape into high speed memory so that the program could run at a higher speed. This creates a sort of a layered system of memory combining both slow and fast memory. Today's computers use this layered approach concept extensively.

1.8 The UNIVAC 1105's operating system

The UNIVAC 1105 was produced with an operating system—of sorts—if you could call it such. Rather than have the operating system remaining in high speed memory as it is today, the 1105 had a somewhat unique technique to maximize the amount of high speed memory available to the programmer. As mentioned earlier, the 1105 at ARF had 8,192 words of core memory; about the equivalent of 32,768 8-bit bytes. Today a programmer could easily go out of his or her mind if they had to write any significant program to fit into something so small. A few lines of text in a modern word processor program like Microsoft Word or Apple's Pages would fill the entire memory. It was almost like having to do something constrained in a straight jacket.

The 1105's approach was to reserve 192 of the 8,192 words in core for tightly programmed routines to be brought into memory to perform a specific function like format a value to be printed. Consequently, the operating system just consisted of numerous small programmed routines residing on the drum which were read into the same core memory locations as needed. That was the purpose of having the drum logically divided into the A and B drums. A programmer could do whatever they wanted with the A drum, but it was strictly hands off to mess with the B drum where all these small routines were kept.

Well, I like puzzles and became fairly good at looking at the octal contents of an instruction word and working backwards to figure out what a routine was supposed to do.[5] It's like programming in reverse. Consequently I became very curious about all the routines in drum B. One of the routines was a core dump that dumped out all the contents of the locations in core memory—in octal of course—so a programmer could find programming bugs.

There was also a routine to dump the contents of the drum, either A or B, so that it may be printed out. The selection of which drum to dump was controlled by a two push button switches on the console. One time I inconspicuously backed up to the console, and unobserved by the operator, pushed the button so that a dump of drum B would be made. I took the listing, perhaps three quarters of an inch thick, back to my office and started pouring over it, decoding the routines used and how they were structured. Then digging through the 1105's manual, I found that I could programmatically switch between drums A and B at will.

I was never content with how some of the stored routines worked— they might produce a format I thought could be tweaked—and so I wrote some code by which I could modify the contents of drum B to make slight modifications to existing routines. In essence what I was doing would today be called "hacking" but back then they didn't have a name for it.

After I would finish my work on the computer, subsequent users started to complain that the 1105 was not acting right. It didn't take a genius to put one and one together and get the result of me being the source of the problem. Consequently whenever I would get finished with my work, a computer operator would routinely replace the contents of drum B to what it should be. Since I was paying $650 per hour—a good paying customer—no one ever stopped me from trying new tricks on the machine.

From that time on, I've always felt the programmer is the master and if I could push the hardware to accomplish what I wanted, no matter how thwarted my desires were, I would push a computer to its limits. Years later I would even rewire some circuit boards to bend the computer to do my bidding. I would go where other computer people normally wouldn't approach with a ten-foot pole.

---

[5] See section A.2 on page 151 for more details on number bases.

1.9 Programming the UNIVAC 1105

Titles for computer workers depend on who is doing the classification. In my mind I generally follow the following job designations. *Hardware engineers* are usually technical people who are electrical engineers who understand the inner workings of the physical hardware. These are the workers who work from the electrical schematics of the computer's wiring.

And then there are the *programmers*. I divide programmers into two overall groups; the first being *systems programmers*. Systems programmers handle low-level coding for machines. They program and work on operating systems where essential knowledge of a computer's hardware architecture is required. They keep the computer running smoothly and implement features to make higher level user applications easier to use. They also write such things as compilers that translate higher level languages into a form that the computer understands.

The other main type of programmers are the *applications programmers*. I subdivide this class into two basic subdivisions: *scientific application programmers* and *commercial applications programmers*. Scientific applications programmers generally are scientists and engineers that use computers for scientific and engineering problem solving. Commercial applications programmers do programming directed toward commercial applications.

System designers or *systems analysts* are higher level people who know a particular application well and use this knowledge to design an overall system to accomplish the specific task at hand. In summary it should be recognized that there are no hard and fast divisions separating any of the above classifications. Very often a single person can be doing several different tasks simultaneously. I've met application programmers that were challenged by system designing. And I've met system analysts who couldn't program their way out of a wet paper sack if their life depended on it. Consequently I don't label a person by their title but rather by their ability in different areas of the work involved.

My general philosophy has always been to become versatile in all areas involving computers. Based on my career in computer technology, I've always found it most useful—and appreciated by employers—to become a jack of all trades in each of the areas above. Today the tendency is for people to concentrate on one area. I see nothing wrong with this except, in my opinion, that is sort of boxing oneself into a narrow area of expertise. By the time I retired I had experience all the way from designing electronic circuits and circuit boards to programming complete operating systems to doing both commercial and scientific programming and even web applications. My specialty became problem solving when a problem arose that nobody else had been able to solve, a so-called last resort if you will. I attribute most of this to my intrinsic curiosity of how things work at the lowest level, a trait I've had for as long as I can remember. The only difference between way back when and now is that now I can can successfully put together what I've taken apart to find out how it works.

1.10 Computer programming

Computer programming is not a one-size-fits-all proposition. Each machine has what is referred to as a *machine language*; this is the language that the machine itself knows how to interpret and execute. The vast majority of programmers today do not program in machine language because it is not efficient—from the programmer's viewpoint—to do so. Systems programmers, like myself, used to program at this level because it is the closest level to the actual machine itself and hence I could squeeze out every bit of the raw power of the machine. I could program a tighter, smaller, and faster application in machine language than in most higher level programming languages.

Except for a scattering of applications that were more suitable to be programmed in higher level languages, most of the work I did up to the 1985 time period was done at this lower level language. Programming at this low level one needed to know the architecture of a machine in bloody detail. There were tricks that a person could use for efficiency that just weren't available with a higher level language.

One major disadvantage of programming in a low level language was that the program could not easily be converted to run on a different computer. And also it was confusing for other programmers who were brought up with other higher level languages to cope with machine language. My brother, for example, excelled at scientific programming—the likes of which I could never duplicate—and would rather face the wrath of the devil before writing in machine language.

There were a plethora number of higher level languages to make pro-

1.10 Computer programming   23

gramming easier starting in the 1950s. Even the IBM 650 had such a language called SOAP. During the decades of the 50s and 60s, many programming languages were developed both for scientific and commercial purposes. In the scientific arena the big early language was FORTRAN in which a line of FORTRAN coding echoed the format one would use in writing an equation, e.g., $A = B + C$. In machine language to duplicate this one must first load a register with the contents of storage location B then add the number stored in location C to the register and finally store the result in location A. In general one line of a FORTRAN program might typically require 10 or 20 lines if written in machine language. This was good for engineers but removed the programmer further and further from the actual machine hardware itself.

One of the early commercial languages was COBOL. I hated to program in COBOL where a typical line of code might be written as "UPDATED-INVENTORY-ON-HAND equals ITEM-INVENTORY-ON-HAND minus INVENTORY-SOLD" or the likes of this. It was great for business people but took the programmer even further from the actual machine itself. Huge names were possible to represent a number in a memory locations and I found it tedious to type out a program like I'd write a long letter to someone.

I simply referred to myself proudly as a "bit diddler." Whenever an application required fast execution times I was called upon to write it because of my experience with writing in machine language. Few programmers I ever worked with wrote at this level. To me, speed was important and hence I preferred to write in machine language.

The 1105 came with a good machine language *assembler* called USE. Each line of code produced a single machine level instruction. When writing in machine language it was almost impossible to write in actual machine language itself which was just a string of octal or hexadecimal characters representing operation codes and physical addresses in memory. An assembler's job was to translate a readable name like "field1" into the actual memory location address which might be "37652." Then if a change in logic was required, the computer itself would keep track of, and dynamically change, a readable name into something the machine would understand.

The 1105 also came with a *compiler*, UNIVAC's version of a FORTRAN type engineering language called *Internal Translator* or IT. The compiler itself was quite buggy. Luckily each line of IT programming was shown in the listing as to what machine language was produced to execute that line of code.

It was quite handy to know the actual machine language. I remember one time I took two weeks off to study for some upcoming college exams. One of the ARF computer department programmers was helping me on a coding project I was working on. When I got back to work, he told me that the program was not working as expected and he was frustrated at not getting the expected results. He had checked and double checked his logic and was absolutely sure that his logic was flawless. I took a quick look at the machine language produced by his line of IT programming produced after compilation and realized the compiler had a bug in it.

This sort of thing has happened on numerous occasions over the years. The computer is perhaps, in my opinion, the most perfect creation man has ever developed. It does exactly what it is told to do. Exactly! The trouble is that what it is told to do most times was wrong. I mention this because I have run into situations where a hardware component had failed, and the machine's execution of a particular machine language instruction itself did not work as it should. In these situations an applications programmer was just in over his or her head.

One other thing that should be mentioned at this point was who was considered the "expert." I observed that a programmer's boss frequently considers themself to know more about programming than what the programmer does.[6] They know best as to what the priorities of program development should be. I generally ignored such advice preferring to program the way it "should" be done. If I anticipated a later change to a program that would be hard to incorporate later because of the logic involved, I would take the extra 5% time to take such anticipated change into account. This step saved my posterior time and again.

1.11 Applications

At ARF I was in the hydrodynamics group and worked mostly on the Atomic Energy Commission (AEC) project. I generally divided my time between our laboratory and my office when I was programming. When the UNIVAC 1105 was first installed, one of the engineers for the system

---

[6]The exception to this is when the boss is an experienced programmer, but even then I may question their logic.

1.11 Applications

gave two 2-hour classes on the machine. I attended both, got loaded up with a stack of manuals, and by the end was more confused than before I took the classes. In those days there were no college courses in computers—perhaps MIT had some but most colleges and universities didn't—so one must learn by just reading the manuals. A few years later IIT did offer such a course but it was in programming an IBM 1620 commercial machine which, after working on the 1105, was more like programming a handheld calculator rather than a machine where one could do some serious work.

Loving to play with the 1105, I did considerable "playing" around with the machine. The first application I wrote—if one could call it that—was to analyze the distance my fingers would move on a standard typewriter keyboard compared with the distance on a Dvorak keyboard. The Dvorak keyboard was the product of a naval contract during World War II with the goal of making typing more efficient. The key layout was much different than a standard keyboard based on letter frequency rather than a random pattern like on the qwerty keyboard.

Once I had a "feel" for the UNIVAC, my boss Paul thought it would be a good idea for me to write a program, based on his technical knowledge of hydrodynamics, to do the tedious calculations for shock wave motion. This was to attempt to theoretically model the experiments we were doing on the strong shock tube. The AEC bought the idea and provided sub-project funds to work on such a program.

I did an analysis to determine how I could adapt the problem to a workable program. In the laboratory we would take sample materials, mostly woods of different types that we knew the pressure versus volume characteristics of, put these samples at the end of the shock tube, and hit them with high pressure shock waves. As the samples crushed very rapidly under strong shock waves, we would use specialized gauges to measure the pressure versus time of the shock waves as they propagated through the crushing samples. This was the type of data reduction I was initially hired to do.

Some substances like water or steel could not be compressed very much, but porous materials like wood would be crushed to a high extent. If we could model this crushing using a computer program then we could try various combinations of materials to see which ones make the best blast shields. None of the other engineers in our hydrodynamics group knew anything about programming so it was up to me to do program development. With today's high level languages, the task would be fairly easy, but we had no high level language on the 1105 except IT and that, being too buggy, was clearly not up to the task. Hence I decided to write the code in assembler, i.e., machine language. I was making nice progress on the task, but this was not fast enough for my superiors—remember, one's superiors always think they know better how programs should be written than the programmers.

After many argumentative discussions, I finally agreed to write the program using the IT compiler. We ran into problems galore because the IT language was not up to the task. After the length of time being spent increased substantially, I began to wonder if it was worth the effort. About that time, the early 1960s, ARF, now called IITRI, brought in another computer: an IBM 7094. This new machine was a transistorized scientific computer which still had a 36-bit word length, but it was much faster and did have a FORTRAN compiler.

While I had most of the logic worked out for the program, it was suggested that we get a couple of people from the computer department to help me transfer the logic to FORTRAN. This was agreed to so I would essentially write out the logic needed on a blackboard, and my two helpers would write down the logic in FORTRAN. This worked fairly well except that the people helping would make typing mistakes when punching cards—the 7094 used cards instead of paper tape—because they were relying on the computer to find their programming errors which didn't work much of the time. As we approached 2,000 cards for the program, most of my time was spent debugging the code because I knew the physical problem we were trying to solve. I believed I could have done the job much faster by myself rather than getting others involved and still do.

One of the fallacies I've found over and over with computer work is that non-computer oriented managers think that the more people on a job equates to the job being completed sooner. There have been studies on this topic; one such study was published in a book titled *The Mythical Man-month* that indicates that this approach is not always the best to take. Just because an assembly line in a factory might be able to produce increases in output doesn't mean that putting more programmers on a task does likewise especially for complex tasks. Time and again over my career I have run into this situation. I sarcastically maintain that everyone's a genius, just ask them!

1.11 Applications

After an inordinate period of time, I finally got the program done. I called it my SWIMM code meaning Stress Waves In Multilayered Media (see Figure 1.15). I documented it in a long final report which is, the last time I looked, available somewhere in the government archives. It was quite an extensive program that could configure a blast shield consisting of up to 40 layers of different materials, each having a different thickness. Then an emulated arbitrary-shaped shock wave would impact the shield resulting in a complex pattern of internal shock waves which crushed the shield. To be able to model this on a computer, rather than in an experimental laboratory, provided rapid simulated testing of various shield designs. I was quite proud of the final result.

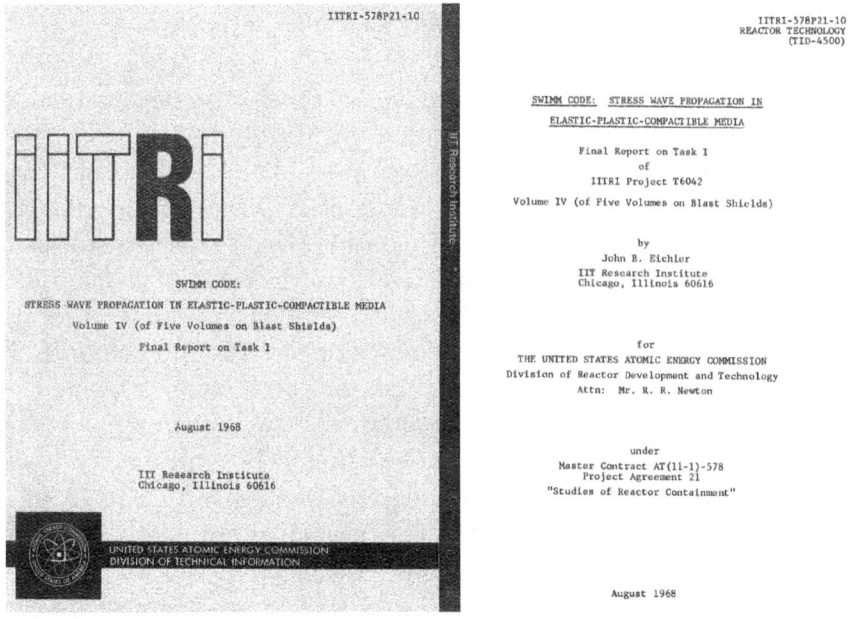

Figure 1.15: The cover and title page of my SWIMM code final report to the Atomic Energy Commission. (SOURCE: From my copy of the report. Available from U.S. government archives.)

There were two other computer programs for the UNIVAC 1105 I wrote while at IITRI I'm quite proud of also. One was a code-tracing program to help find bugs in a computer program. I wrote this application in assembly language, and its purpose was quite simple. It would take an arbitrary other computer program and execute it step-by-step giving a printout of all the instructions in the order executed in the other program. When loops were found in the analyzed program it would tell the number of times the loop was executed in the output listing. This tracing program could probably be called a "systems program" since it would work on arbitrary other programs to help debugging logic. Today there are other helper mechanisms on various systems, but this logic trace program was written to work on a vacuum tube early generation mainframe and the first such program I had ever heard of.

The other program I wrote was something quite new and experimental for a vacuum tube machine. The reason I'm proud of this second application was that I think I was one of the first people to ever develop such a program. And it was written at a time when computers were relatively new and most engineers were not able to interact with them easily.

Around 1963 transistors were coming into their own, and some new digital equipment was beginning to come out using them. The new IBM 7094 was coming into more widespread use at IITRI. This meant that most of the people that used the 1105 migrated to the 7094 leaving the 1105 much less frequently used. As a result the 1105 was being used more and more as a development machine, and the engineers responsible for it were interested in doing experimental work on it. Part of this work was to attach new equipment to the machine and play around with it. Coupled with this was the introduction of new programming techniques with one such technique allowing programmers to develop applications wherein a program could be executed as it was being written.

Some programmers in IITRI's computer department heard of such systems being developed by others as experimental projects elsewhere in the country. They wanted to get in on the action, and so the computer department had the UNIVAC engineers install some new specialized equipment on the machine. Remember this was years before the development of the computer mouse and the modern display terminals. Almost all computer processing was done as *batch processing* where programmers had to type their programs that resulted in either a paper tape or IBM cards being produced. They then turned in their coded tape or cards to the computer department and operators would run the program and give the programmer back a listing of their output. The programmers would not be the ones to run the actual computer.

Being able to sit at the computer and actually type in a program and

1.11 Applications

test it out immediately—like can be done today—was not possible. Consequently the 1105 engineers installed three analog-to-digital and three digital-to-analog converters to the system. Analog signals are essentially signals where a continuous variable voltage signal rather than a digital, i.e., where 0s and 1s, are used. Up to the time of the digital revolution, analog signals were prevalent. Some early computers, called analog computers, were developed but eventually the digital computers made them obsolete except in specialized applications. The analog-to-digital converters were used to convert an analog voltage level to its digital equivalent, i.e., a digital value that could be used in computations. The digital-to-analog converters did the opposite. They took a digital value and converted it into a output voltage level. These were cool devices that today are used extensively and called A/D and D/A converters.

To rig a terminal to display some sort of pattern, the engineers used an oscilloscope where a point could be displayed as a dot on the face of the display. To display a series of dots very rapidly, which the computer could easily do, I was able to draw a graphic on the face of the oscilloscope. The position of a dot displayed on the face of the oscilloscope was only dependent on a voltage level in the x-direction and a voltage level in the y-direction. If one was able to write dots continuously on the scope, a pattern could be obtained. Under the control of the computer, appropriate patterns representing characters and digits could be displayed on the face of the oscilloscope. This was the stone-age equivalent of the modern graphics display terminals with which we are all familiar today.

I was quite familiar with oscilloscopes having used them in the laboratory. (See Figure 1.3.) In the lab we would set the x-value to be produced by the oscilloscope itself based on time. The y-value would be determined by the input voltage from a pressure gauge on the shock tube producing a pressure versus time trace recorded on a Polaroid picture of the face of the oscilloscope. This is roughly the same as a picture produced on an old television. The terminal worked on the same principle except now the input voltage would be driven by the computer outputting digital values for x and y and putting these values through the digital-to-analog converters.

For input values to the computers—remember the mouse hadn't been invented yet—the engineers made a square pad that had a small vertical plastic piece that was connected by strings to pulleys on all 4 corners. Movement of the plastic piece moved the strings which underneath the pad were connected to variable resistors that produced analog voltages in both the x and y directions. In essence, it was a stone-age mouse precursor. These voltages would be fed into two analog-to-digital converters, and hence the computer could use the digital output to tell where the plastic piece was on the pad.

When I saw this jerry-rigged system in operation, an idea came to me. Rather than use the laboratory oscilloscopes in a shock tube experiment, why not just record the voltage variations on a analog magnetic tape—like one would tape record the output of a microphone—and have the computer do the analog-to-digital conversion? Such a system could do away with the recording of the pressure wave versus time on a Polaroid photo; this would work much better.

Figure 1.16: Me at the jerry-rigged terminal for the UNIVAC 1105.
(SOURCE: Picture taken for an article in IITRI's *Frontier* magazine for spring 1967 edition.)

Figure 1.16 is a picture of this system with me using the system for

1.11 Applications

testing. My left hand was on a small box having 16 buttons. When a button was pressed it sent a signal to the UNIVAC indicating which button was activated. I programmed the 1105 to do a different function on the waveform for each button. My right hand is on our *pseudo* mouse. The pulleys at the corners that the strings went around to the variable resistors on the underside of the square box. Even though I could detect an x and y position of the little plastic cylinder I moved with my hand, I was only interested in the x position which I fed back as a vertical line on the display. For the purpose of putting something on the screen for this picture, I just put a computer-generated sine wave to show the idea. The actual pressure wave forms from the experiment looked way different.

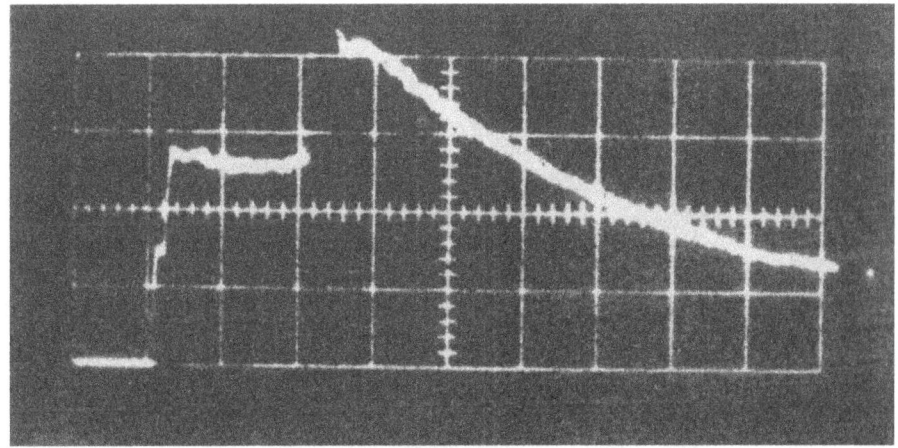

Figure 1.17: A Polaroid picture of the type that is to be displayed.
(SOURCE: From one of IITRI's reports to the AEC.)

Shown in Figure 1.17 is an actual pressure versus time trace typical of the kind that I did manual data reduction on. The total trace, i.e., 10 horizontal boxes represents 5 milliseconds (five thousands of a second). The computer digitizes this data 20 times per horizontal box or about 200 samplings over the entire 5 milliseconds shown. The pressure at this gauge station was low initially (first horizontal box flat line) and then it rose to about the 2 box level when the shock wave hit the sample (second and third horizontal boxes) crushing the wood sample under test. Finally the pressure tops out (last half of the fourth box) and starting about the beginning of the fifth box when the wood is compressed fully and, starting about the beginning of the fifth horizontal box, the pressure gradually falls off. As you might guess, making all these measurements by hand was the pits but for a computer to do it was a dream.

Then to analyze the data manually, I used the experimental terminal system to analyze the data "online." I could display the pressure waveform on the oscilloscope and use the "mouse" to select different portions of the wave to work on. This way an engineer, knowing nothing about computers, could sit at the terminal and analyze the data directly. I proposed my idea to the guys I worked with back in the hydrodynamic lab, and everyone thought it would be a great way to rapidly do an accurate analysis of the experimental output. It was something new and different and, to the best of my knowledge, had never been tried before. I got the go-ahead to develop such a system. I was elated!

Figure 1.18: An Ampex commercial tape unit similar in shape to the one we used but not the same model. (SOURCE: Original source is unknown but probably Ampex.)

1.11 Applications

We needed a 14-channel professional grade tape recorder that recorded on 1 inch wide tape. It turned out that IITRI had such a unit similar to the one shown in Figure 1.18.[7] It was big and very heavy so we found a rollable cart to put it on. The experiment took place in building 16 (see Figure 1.1), and the computer was located in building 24 so we had to transport the recorder back and forth between the two buildings for each experimental run.

On 13 of the 14 channels available the actual analog data from the pressure gauges were recorded. On the 14th channel we recorded a constant frequency sine wave. The engineers at the UNIVAC rigged up a Schmidt-trigger that gave a signal at every zero crossing of the sine wave. This, in essence, was like having a clock signal on the tape itself instructing the computer to sample the data at exact time intervals. This was necessary since the computer only had 3 channels of analog-to-digital conversion available so it required several passes of the analog tape to read in all 13 data channels. Using these zero crossings ensured that samples were always taken at the exact same instant. In this manner we were able to rerun the tape several times in order to get all 13-channel time-correlated experimental data into the 1105. In other words, there would be no time slew between all data channels.

Today virtually all computers have what is known as an *interval timer* which interrupts the computer at set time intervals. The UNIVAC 1105 did not have such a hardware feature which provided a programming challenge. This meant that I had to figure out some way to emulate a timer via software in my input code. There was no way on the 1105 could digitize in realtime so we recorded the data at 60 inches per second and played it back at 1 7/8 inches per second so that time would be stretched out. This means that my input program had to get back to get the next sample at exactly every 800 microseconds.

Since I knew the exact number of microseconds each computer instruction took, I figured I could write an input routine that looped to take the next sample at the time required. There was no way to write the

---

[7] I should not have been surprised at this since an electrical engineer named Marvin Camras who worked for ARF/IITRI worked in the same physics building that housed the UNIVAC. He held over 500 patents primarily in the field of magnetic recording and was considered the father of both wire and tape recording devices. Unfortunately, at the time I worked for IITRI, I never had a chance to meet him in person, but now wish I had looked him up.

incoming data to the drum because it was far too slow for the process, so I decided to use tape as buffer storage. But using one tape drive was also too slow for the incoming data. Luckily the 1105 had two tape control units (TCUs), one for each of the two banks of digital tape drives. So I wrote one buffer of 120 words to one TCU and then filled a core buffer with the next 120 words that I could send to the other TCU and ping-pong back and forth writing each 120 block of data such that each tape contained exactly half of the data.

One of the top systems programmers—the guru of the department—did some calculations and was convinced there was no way on earth that I could write out the data fast enough to a single tape buffer. I bet him $5 that I could sample fast enough not telling him that was going to use two tapes on separate TCUs to do the job. He erred by assuming I was going to use only one tape drive. I won the bet, but he never paid up when my system worked.

Another way I tested my input program was to connect a variable sine wave generator to the input that the output from the Schmidt trigger was going to use.[8] In this way I could crank up the frequency of the sine wave until the computer program eventually stopped. This was how I made sure that my scheme would work. Because my code had it's hands full with dumping one buffer to a TCU while filling another buffer to write to the other TCU, I had to ensure that all the logic paths in my program were timed such that I would be back at exactly 800 microseconds to read the next digitized 3 channels of data. It worked even though in some logic program paths I had to insert dummy instructions just to take some time such that all paths took exactly the same amount of

---

[8]Initially all I knew about a Schmidt trigger was that it detected zero-crossing from the control signal we recorded on one of the tracks using a sine wave. Fifteen years later when I was designing digital circuitry I got to know the Schmidt trigger very well because it is so widely used in electronics. I attended a computerized electrocardiogram conference in Banff, Canada, where the keynote speaker was Professor Otto Schmidt who invented the Schmidt trigger as a graduate student in 1938 or thereabouts. It was a great opportunity for me, and I must have talked to him for nearly two hours. We flew back to Denver on the same plane and talked more at the Denver airport. He was a fascinating individual and quite a character. It also turned out that Schmidt was a good friend to Dr. Edwin Land, inventor of the plastic Polaroid filter and the Polaroid camera. Schmidt told me of a famous demonstration Land did wherein he purposely had his wife drop a slide on the floor to give an optimal delay time for the eyes of his audience so they would get the best effect for his color demonstration. I'll never forget meeting Schmidt at that conference.

time. It worked like clockwork.

Since the data read in from the analog tape was done so using multiple passes and written out to two different physical digital computer tapes, it was necessary to put together all this data in a sorted form. I wrote a couple of other programs that read in the blocks from each digital tape and put the data back into proper order. This sorted data was then written to the drum such that my final program to display the waveform did so effortlessly and optimally. By slowing the playback of the data on the Ampex unit by a factor of 32 I was able to digitize the experimental data so that I was able to sample points that were originally 25 microseconds apart which was more than enough to do the analysis.

Of all the programming that I did at IITRI I think this was my favorite task. I had done something that, to the best of my knowledge, had never been done before anywhere.

1.12 The IBM 7094

While I was working on the system just described on the UNIVAC 1105, I found myself also tiding up my SWIMM code. The main difference between the two computers was that on the UNIVAC, because so few people used that machine, I could operate the machine myself, and therefore could debug my program as I worked on it. On the other hand, with the IBM 7094 I had to type my program on IBM cards and submit them to be run by the operators. Anyone who has ever worked in a batch processing environment will tell you that the turn-around time is a killer. You'd submit the job early in the morning and many times have to wait until the afternoon to get the results. If an error had occurred even so small as a misplaced comma, the programmer would have to fix the error and resubmit the program that afternoon or the next day and go through the whole process again. It's a real pain to program that way especially if you have someone breathing down your neck for any deadline.

The 7094 had a "real" operating system if you could call it that. The machine had more memory—I believe it was either 32,768 (32K) or 65,536 (64K) words—and it was all transistorized. Programs ran fast on the machine. I don't remember what the hourly charge was for the machine, but they probably charged by the minute. The operating system was called IBSYS and remained in core memory which sped things up. This system was an early attempt to optimize batch processing. Still no realtime facilities were available on this machine. I don't remember much about the innards of the 7094 because I never programmed the machine in assembly language but rather wrote all the programs in FORTRAN. It, like the UNIVAC 1105, used 36-bit words and was an octal machine.

One interesting aspect of the 7094 system was that IITRI had rented two IBM 1401 computers to be used only for input and output. The 1401 was a commercial transistorized machine designed more for business applications and was a very popular small machine. The rental cost of the 1401 started about $2,500 per month and hence smaller medium-sized businesses could afford to have one. The 1401 read in the cards and wrote them out to a magnetic tape. This made it possible to put multiple programs to a single magnetic digital tape which was manually transported to the 7094. The IBSYS operating system took care of the batching which also sped up the operation. The machine wrote all the output to another digital tape which was manually taken to one of the 1401s for printing.

Figure 1.19: The IBM 7094 transistorized scientific mainframe computer.
(SOURCE: Original source is unknown but this photo was from Columbia University.)

In the early 1960s computers were roughly divided into scientific word-oriented mainframes and smaller character-oriented machines of which the 1401 was a good example. The 1401's memory stored characters of 7-bit length plus one *parity* bit. Most machines included a parity check bit—even the 36-bit word machines—that served as a check on whether a memory location contained a valid value. Upon each memory access the hardware circuitry would check to see if the total number of 1 bits in the fetched data added up to be either odd or even depending on the actual machine. Since memory at that time was not always reliable, such a check would indicate the validity of the data from that memory location.

With character-oriented machine some mechanism was needed to tell where a number stopped. Hence one of the 7-bits was a flag bit which told where the number ended. The remaining 6 bits could hold a total of 64 possible values (2^6) which is somewhat limiting. Because IITRI had a couple of 1401s, I couldn't resist the challenge to see if I could program it. I soon gave up after reading the 1401 manuals because it was a little too messy even for my tastes.

In the mid 1960s, IBM gave up on building two different types of machines—commercial and scientific—and came out with IBM 360 computer systems, a complete family of computers based on the 8-bit *byte*. Bytes could be combined as *half-words* having two bytes and *full-words* having four bytes. In this way they could rent machines to both the commercial and scientific markets. Since IITRI didn't have any 360s, I didn't investigate these machines to any extent at the time.

1.13   A few extra comments on IITRI

Before leaving the subject of the time I spent working at IITRI, I'd like to mention two individuals I met there who were, in my opinion, exceptional. The first was Fran Porzel, the senior scientist in our division. Fran was a hydrodynamic engineer who had done the hydrodynamics calculations for the first hydrogen bomb tests. His speciality was the study of shock waves produced when a bomb exploded and he was well recognized for his expertise.

Fran's office—about the largest in the division—was larger than almost any other. It was located directly across the hall from my office. He was an interesting individual because of his wide range of interests. Many afternoons after I was burned out on programming (I always did most of my work in the mornings when my mind was functioning on all eight cylinders). About two or three in the afternoon I would wander across the hall to see if Fran was busy and if he wasn't I'd go in and we'd have fantastic discussions on a whole range of topics, none about work. Fran had a large family and would leave work and jump on a train taking him home. On many occasions we'd get so involved in our discussions that he'd look at his watch and would realize he had stayed too long after hours and would take off to catch his last train home. After I left IITRI, I heard that Fran moved to Washington, D.C., to work for DARPA, the Defense Advanced Research Projects Agency.

The other exceptional individual I met was Ed Murry who headed up the hydrodynamics laboratory where I spent much time in doing experiments (see Figure 1.3). Ed was an expert in electronics design and could instrument nearly anything. He was the "go to" person who most of the engineers would seek out when designing a new experiment. Ed had been in the armed services during World War II in Europe and was considered an absolute genius in radar. Toward the end of the war he was one of the people who had the responsibility for keeping all the radars in the European theater functioning properly.

After the war he was involved with the rebuilding of Europe especially Germany. Ed had a keen interest in how the human mind works. While in Germany he worked with a few medical doctors to see if he could instrument a human's physiological processes in the same manner he could instrument an experiment. His dabbling was fascinating to me since in college I had a minor in psychology, a subject I had been keenly interested in since high school days. We became close friends and would spend hours together in the lab after everyone else went home. Ed had married a French woman who was a fantastic chef, a fact I can attest to.

Ed didn't know much about computers except in general terms. Since I did, we talked about how a computer could emulate human thought, and I was deeply interested in that idea. Ed would explain in detail his experiments in *psychotherapy* that he had performed with the doctors in Germany. This kindled my interest even more and started a life-long quest of mine into the subject. I knew that it should be possible to make a computer respond like a human through programming, but my real interest was in the actual mechanism the brain uses for memory storage and retrieval, not the emulation of it by software.

In 1967 I still was one of the few people in our division who was deeply involved in programming. I decided it was time to move on especially because I wanted to get my hands "dirty" and get some commercial experience.

2

Boise Cascade days

My father was a retail merchant in Dixon, Illinois, my hometown, a town of about 15,000 residents. His business, *Eichler Brothers, Inc.*, had one large store in Dixon and a second much smaller one in Amboy, about 13 miles south of Dixon. The business was founded in 1891 by my grandfather and his brother. I always wanted to follow in my father's footsteps and had applied several times for a position as a management trainee at some of the larger retail stores in Chicago. It always turned out that I was "over qualified" and made about twice the money that they could afford to pay me as a trainee.

My father had worked all his life at the store and was of retirement age. He knew well how difficult retailing could be and didn't want either myself or my younger brother to get into it. When he was young and had an opportunity to join some of his classmates who wanted to open an investment banking firm in New York, his father, who was from the old country in Europe, said it was a son's duty to continue in the family business. Even though he became a successful merchant, most of those opportunistic classmates became multimillionaires. He deeply regretted going into the store and surely did not want his sons doing the same. He said the future for us was to work for some large corporation and not make the same mistake he did. Nevertheless, I always wanted to follow in his footsteps.

2.1   My search for a new position

In the spring of 1967 I scanned the want ads in the newspaper for a new opportunity. I ended up getting two job offers in the Chicago area. One was with United Airlines who was installing a new UNIVAC 1108 computer, a newer transistorized version of the 1105. They wanted me based on my extensive knowledge of the UNIVAC computer. I knew it would be a very challenging job that I could do well with my background.

The other position was with Boise Cascade, a huge corporation in the lumber and paper business. They had on order an IBM 360/model 30 for one of their subsidiaries headquartered in Chicago. The subsidiary in Chicago was Horder Office supplies. They had a number of stores around the area and were similar to an Office Depot type retailer. Their computer was to be located at the corner of Jefferson and Jackson streets just above a Horders store on the ground level in downtown Chicago just to the west of the famous Chicago "loop." Their offer would give me a chance to get my hands dirty in the field of retailing, which I had long desired, so I took that job rather than the one at United.

I knew nothing about the IBM 360 computer but figured I could get up to speed on the machine just from reading a number of IBM manuals which Boise gave me. By that time I was familiar enough with computers to easily follow almost any manual thrown at me. Boise had already hired a number of commercial programmers but lacked a good systems person who could master the internals of the machine for which I was game. I left IITRI and headed for a new experience with Boise. Most of the applications programmers were programming in COBOL. For my part, they didn't want me to program in COBOL but rather in assembler which pleased me greatly.

After accepting the job, I stayed on with IITRI for close to a month to finish up writing my final report on the SWIMM code. I also ran several test blast shield designs through the program and came to the conclusion that the best way to contain an internal explosion was using a thick shield comprised of lead backed by styrofoam or balsa wood and then an exterior container probably made of concrete. The explosion would start the lead moving outward absorbing the momentum of the blast and then be slowed down by the crushing of the styrofoam against the outside vessel. The whole idea, in my mind, was to take the high energy of the blast, which was in milliseconds, and spread that energy

2.1 My search for a new position

over a longer time at a much lower pressure that the concrete vessel could successfully contain.

In the meantime, I digested about an 8-inch high stack of IBM 360 manuals Boise gave me to read and get up to speed. Their new computer was not due until after my arrival which gave me some time to do this. Figure 2.1 shows a typical IBM 360/model 30 installation similar to what ours would be. Ours was scheduled to arrive just before Memorial Day.

Figure 2.1: An IBM 360/model 30 computer system. (SOURCE: Original source unknown but likely IBM Corporation.)

The application programmers were busy writing their COBOL programs and testing them on a 360 system at IBM headquarter in downtown Chicago. I always regarded IBM as standing alone as the big guy in the room and referred to their headquarters as "the Ministry of Truth," a reference to Orwell's book *1984*. "Big brother" was always IBM.

IBM's System 360 consisted of a range of computers with the model 20 being an entry level machine. The models 30, 40, 50, 65, 75, and 91 were part of an upward migration path as IBM would try to push companies into adding new equipment. Their objective was always to rent more and more equipment to their captured market, and they were very successful doing it. The larger machines were quite powerful and filled the gap as scientific processors. They wanted a compatible series of machines to enable their customers to grow without the major expense of having to redo the programs as time went on. It was a wholly logical approach and I give them a lot of credit for consolidating their commercial and scientific machines into one continuum.

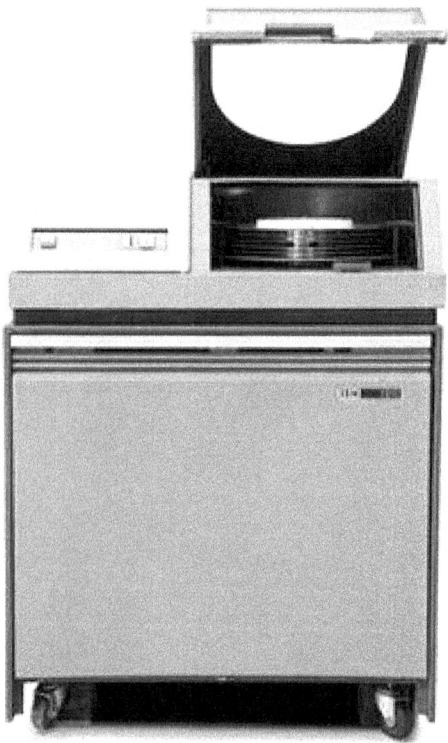

Figure 2.2: An IBM 1311 hard disk storage unit. This unit would store a whopping 2.5 million bytes of data (about the size of a single digital picture today). (SOURCE: Original source unknown but likely IBM Corporation.)

The model 30 introduced me to a couple of new things. First, their high speed printers were attached to the mainframe directly and didn't require the clunky electronics support needed for the 1105 printer. Second, it introduced me to a new device called a storage disk. We had—I believe it was 3—disk drives as shown in Figure 2.2. And, of course, was punched card input and output. No more paper tape! It had a raised floor but no serious air conditioner like the 1105 required. The machine was entirely transistor based. Oh yes, the attached keyboard console was usable as a needed input device for the operator to communicate with the operating system unlike the UNIVAC.

The size of the disk units—although tiny compared to today's trillion-byte storage—was large enough to do some interesting things. But the storage access as provided by IBM. was primitive. One could do a sequential read of data—similar to reading a tape—or set up a data indexing system but that was it. As a systems programmer I could, through assembly language programming, randomly access any portion of the disk which left open some imaginative opportunities.

There were two operating systems for the System 360. One was called the Disk Operating System (DOS) for smaller systems like models 20 and 30. Then there was Operating System (OS) for the higher-end big systems. We affectionately called OS "Big OZ." Boise had a system model 50 or 60 at their headquarters in Boise, Idaho. We were just the new kid on the block. But DOS did support true *multiprocessing*, the ability to run multiple programs concurrently rather than in batch processing mode. Although under OS the number of tasks running concurrently was large in number, DOS only had one foreground and one background program capability.

One very interesting aspect of DOS was that the operating system was generated through one macro instruction. A macro was a block of code that would be produced and tailored to the specific needs of the installation. This was neat! And considering that it would be one of my tasks to maintain the operating system, this was very handy. One would write a kernel program consisting of just a few cards, and the computer itself would generate the entire operating system from this simple input. IBM had both a card reader, a card punch, and a card reader/punch available for the machine depending on customer needs. Boise chose the reader/punch which was less expensive than separate units.

2.2 Showing the 360 who was its new master

Shortly after I arrived at the new job so did the new machine. The IBM field engineer ("FE" in IBM-speak) told me that he would have it operational on the last work day before the Memorial Day weekend.

Memorial Day was on Tuesday that year; this was just a few years before it was changed to Monday each year. This was ideal since I could spend all of the long 4-day weekend learning to tame the new beast. I was intrigued to watch how he did it. Sure enough on the afternoon after installation was complete, the smiling and cheerful young FE showed up with about a 3-inch stack of cards to build the operating system. As it turned out, he told me that he wanted to get it done because the next morning he and his wife were taking an early flight to Montreal, Canada, to visit the Expo 67 going on there.

What the FE didn't realize was that we had a reader/punch rather than just a card reader and separate punch. He put his card deck in the hopper and booted up the system and typed in the appropriate command on the console typewriter to start the operating system generation. The machine read in the first few cards and then punched out another large stack of cards. Unfortunately since we had the reader/punch, the cards punched were over-punched on all the other cards needed to complete the job. When he realized what had happened, he was not a happy camper. IBMers were probably taught not to cuss at the Ministry of Truth, but I'm convinced a string of cuss words went through his mind.

Starting time became later and later and edged into the night. Whenever he suggested that he come back the next week, I reminded him he promised me that the system would be up and running for the weekend. I kept the poor guy until well after midnight. I'm sure he was upset facing a 4:00 a.m. flight just a few hours away. Funny, I never saw him again.

IBM had two card punch machines: a model 026 and a model 029. The difference between the two models was that the 026s could not punch the special characters needed for the 360's operating system. At Boise we had only 026s, the 029s being scheduled to arrive a few weeks later. The commercial applications COBOL programmers in our group didn't run into this problem because they had been keypunching their programs on model 029s at IBM downtown headquarters. But I considered the lack of an 029 a challenge rather than a work stopper. Besides, for those 4 days the building would be empty except for a security guard so there would be no hurry and I could take my time.

I arrived back at work early Saturday morning anxiously waiting until I could get my hands on the new system. Unlike earlier computers I worked on, the 360 had an Initial Program Load (IPL) button that had to be pushed to load in the operating system which resided on one of the disk units. Each of the disk drives held a whopping two and a half million bytes. It was like moving from a no-bedroom apartment into a 50-room mansion. You can imagine my excitement.

So what would I first do on the new machine? It didn't take long to figure out that my first priority would be to make the machine into a three quarter of a million dollar 029 keypunch so I could proceed to do some programming. I remembered in my reading about the machine that there were some utility macros built into the system for handling routine tasks and I figured I could use them to my advantage. Quickly rereading the utilities manual I dived into programming a very simple few line program that would read a line typed on the attached keyboard and then produce a punched card with that line on it and print that line on the high speed printer. Worked like a charm! Now I had a pseudo card punch and could proceed with starting to play with the 360. Over the course of those 4 days I got the hang of the machine and felt very comfortable operating it.

2.3 The first weeks on the model 30

Boise had hired a few operators for the new machine. To train them, the parent corporation in Boise, Idaho, figured it would be a good idea for one of the operators who worked on their large 360 to fly to Chicago to train our new operators. This was good; however, the person they sent was familiar with working with the "Big OZ" operating system on the mainframe back in Boise. He was unfamiliar with DOS so it was a learning experience for him also. All in all, for about a month or so I was about the only person who operated and programmed on the new machine until the model 029 keypunches arrived. This gave me time to produce a listing of the DOS operating system and study it in more detail.

I was quite comfortable with the machine language that DOS was written in and set about seeing what a true multitasking system was all about under the hood. No one else at work had any experience with assembly language so I wrote some assembly language programs and got to know the system assembler and the new instruction formats it presented. It was like a fish taking to water for me.

Boise had decided to input data from their data entry people using teletype machines that produced paper tape. This, of course, was old hat to me... been there, done that. To read in the paper tape, they had rented—from IBM—a paper tape reader that was much different than the small one on the UNIVAC. The reader was about the size of one of the disk drives on the machine. Since this device was a somewhat specialized piece of equipment, I had to write an assembly language program to read in the tape, format the data, and then write out the lines to a disk file for processing by the COBOL applications programs.

Figure 2.3: An IBM 360/model 30 system console. (SOURCE: Original source unknown but likely IBM Corporation.)

One other somewhat new feature to me was that many peripheral devices, i.e., printers, card readers, etc., had "built in" control circuitry. Being familiar with the tape control unit (TCU) on the UNIVAC and how big it was, the migration of control logic to external peripheral de-

2.3 The first weeks on the model 30   47

vices seemed strange back then. But seeing that almost every electronic device is "smart" these days, I guess that was just the start of a trend aided, in most part, by smaller and more sophisticated integrated circuits. The idea was to minimize the work of the central main computer and offload control to the attached peripheral units, a more efficient use of the machine. The computer could then run a program independently of the slower output devices like the printer, card reader, tape drives, and disk drives. One interesting result of this was that hitting the pause button on the main console would pause the running programs and the peripheral devices would keep on running for a period of time before they stopped their activities. I would sometimes play a little trick on the operators by backing up to the system console (see Figure 2.3) and secretly hit the pause button. After a half minute or so the computer would slowly stop all output, and the new operators would have a puzzling look on their faces wondering what had happened. They would ask me what was wrong, and I'd shrug my shoulders with a puzzled look on my face. Then I would hit the pause button again, and the computer would come alive again.

For several months I'd get frantic calls for help from the computer room. The computer would be "acting funny" and so I would go into the computer room and figure out what had gone wrong. One particular morning a call for help came and I went to find out what happened. When I arrived they said to me that the computer would not IPL, i.e., not boot up. Being able to IPL the system was an essential function to load the operating system into memory. Without it the computer would flat out not work. Unlike with the UNIVAC—which was a large enough system to justify having a maintenance engineering staff without having to call in external help—the 360 had only systems programmers like me who were supposed to do magic and get the system working again before calling IBM.

I asked them to hit the IPL button to see what was going on. Whenever a problem happened I would try to see if there was any pattern that might lead me to what was going on. Both the operator from Idaho and our lead operator would take turns hitting the button with nothing happening. The pattern of pushing it seemed to be at random. I thought that maybe the button was acting up so I sat at the console and tried pushing the button myself. The computer did an IPL with no problem. I had the operators try again and still nothing, but every time I tried it the system worked perfectly. I then attempted several iterations between the operators doing it and myself. In every case the computer worked perfectly for me but not for them. It made no sense to me.

So I put on a very stern face and asked them if they told DOS that they loved her. I got strange looks back from everyone. I continued telling them that our little DOS machine probably was acting up because someone from the "Big OZ" environment was there and our machine resented not getting the attention it richly deserved. I suggested that they try to make amends with DOS by treating her better and then left the room. That night after everyone had left I went back in the computer room and typed out a long love letter—telling how DOS was a better operating system than "Big OZ"—on the console typewriter and left it for the operators to see the next morning. Never heard anyone complain about doing IPL after that.[1]

2.4 The project at Boise

One of the primary reasons Boise got the machine was to do billing for their office supply stores. The way they billed was a rather complex process. They had a multitude of different clients in different classifications depending on volume of business they did. Each classification had a range of discounts that had to be applied to their orders. The application programmers ranged in their expertise as to the office supply business. The person who knew the most about the process was a man named Gordon who knew the office supply business backward and forward having worked in it for years and was invaluable to the project. Gordon programmed in COBOL in a "western" style. All the names of his subroutines were like something straight out of

---

[1] Author's note: Over the years I have been working with computers I've encountered this sort of situation more than once. It always leaves a person with an unsolvable problem to ponder. I once read a science fiction story about machines and a guy who found that by looking out the corner of his eye could see supposedly inanimate machines move. The machines so realized that someone would sneakily observed them and ended up killing the guy. I often think of that story when something strange happens with a machine. Even though it sounds a little weird, I've always regarded machines as having personalities and regarded my interaction with them as a challenge to figure out what the problem was as one might do in a challenge between two humans. Naturally, most of the people I've worked with considered me somewhat strange in this regard, but with me it seemed to work.

2.4 The project at Boise

a western movie. "ROUND-THEM-UP," "CUT-THEM-OFF-AT-THE-PASS," and "HEAD-THEM-OUT" were typical examples of his naming scheme. (All names in COBOL were capitalized. In fact, most computers in those day used all caps.) I always got a kick out of the names he would select.

There were a number of programs in the billing system. My initial task was to read in the paper tapes produced by the input operators on the Teletype machines and scan for obvious errors so that clean data were fed to the rest of the system. However, there frequently were keypunch errors that were impossible to detect. The initial programs in the billing data flow would detect a multitude of other errors such as the wrong item or customer number, etc. And then subsequent programs might find other non-obvious errors. This required the keypunch operators to retype the order and re-submit the entire order to the billing system. Some orders were quite long and retyping the entire order was to be avoided from the standpoint of overall efficiency. Hence it was decided that a "suspense" file would be an ideal solution. When the system detected a bad order, it was stored in this file and not processed. Later after corrections were made to the line(s) in error, the corrections were merged with the original order held in the suspense file, the corrected order was re-submitted to the billing system. The main obstacle to this was there were no good way of doing this with the existing IBM supplied software. It was simply too primitive for the job.

I was asked to work out a solution to this problem, i.e., write an organization scheme that would work for this particular application. It should be noted that input orders were of all different lengths and in those days variable length records were not common in file systems, especially with IBM systems. I loved this challenge and set out to develop such a system. For about a week I walked around the place thinking of various schemes to handle this data. When people would ask me what I was doing I would just reply "thinking." On Friday night just before quitting time I came up with a scheme I thought might work. However, I wasn't feeling well and thought I was coming down with the flu or something.

On Saturday I was running a low grade fever but worked out some of the details of my scheme at home in the morning and afternoon. Knowing how important this was to the billing system, I headed down to work about five o'clock in the evening. My routine had to be written in assembly language since any higher level language would not be able to stand up to the task. Besides, I knew tricks to make the suspense file extremely fast. One such trick was after one disk record was fetched, I would send the read/write recording heads to where I was going to fetch the next record from. Head movement was much slower than actual reading of the data so I could process the fetched record while I told the system to move the heads to the next position.

By noontime on Sunday I had written an 850-line assembly program up and running, and it worked like a champ. I used many tricks I learned over the years, and sometimes my logic would get rather complex. One of the things I did was to create a program that would immediately stop if any bad data was detected thereby preventing corruption of the file system. This meant that no maintenance program was needed to fix a corrupted database.[2] Very sophisticated, I thought. It was something new when it came to file systems. Also, I organized the disk to handle different length orders, and once an order had been corrected, it was removed from the file system making room for new records. Eventually when I showed my approach to some IBM software engineers they seemed genuinely impressed by it.

Eventually I was ready to leave Boise for other greener pastures. The week before I left, I got a call in the middle of the night saying the system stopped dead cold. I immediately headed for the office and discovered my programming error. I assigned every order passing though the system what I called a Basic Reference Number (BRN) so that if an operator typing error in the main fields of an order was mistyped, we could still find this specific order to correct because it was accessed using the BRN, a machine-generated value. In IBM assembler language there were two instructions to load a register: a load register instruction (LR) which loaded a 4-byte value and a load address instruction (LA) which load only 3-bytes into the register. I had used the LA instruction instead of LR. Naturally a 4-byte (2^{32}) number could be greater than a 3-byte (2^{24}) value. We had been using the system for months and finally the BRN reached a value of 16 million and my software correctly picked up the logical inconsistency and stopped the processing.

Several months prior to my departure, Boise had hired an assembly

---

[2] I've always tried to make bullet-proof databases. I assume that at any time the power might go off or the computer would be interrupted for some other reason. I therefore write my database code such that any interruption doesn't require any special steps to be taken to restore integrity.

language programmer intended to fill my position. He found my coding convoluted, yet well documented, and in 3-months he never did fully understand what I had programmed. I think that was just due to lack of working at the systems programming level where many "tricks of the trade" are more commonplace. I have always found that programmers tend to program to the level of how complex they think. Even most assembly language programmers are not systems programmers with a deep understanding of things such as operating systems, and hence convoluted schemes by a good systems programmer could scare off the fainthearted. An interesting thing about the file scheme I used, when several years later I visited Boise—now with their bigger 360 system—I was surprised to find them still using my overnight coding file scheme virtually untouched from when I first wrote it.

2.5 Moving on to greener pastures

In the fall of 1967 my mother very suddenly passed away. My father was still working daily in the store but approaching retirement age.

I was still entertaining the idea of wanting to follow in his footsteps. After about 2 years at Boise I started looking around for some position where I could get some experience at management. Like before, I scanned the want ads. Around March, 1969, when I was in the middle of interviewing at some places in the Chicago area, I got a call that my father was in the hospital seriously ill. My brother and I along with our wives drove at breakneck speed the 100 miles back to Dixon only to get there moments before he died. Suddenly I realized that someone either had to take his place in the store or else we had to sell the business. I realized that selling an established family business that had been around since 1891 would be bad. It was the opportunity for me to finally get into a management position just like I sought for years to do. I decided to give up computers and move back to Dixon with my growing family.

3

Dixon Days: Software to Women's wear

The two original brothers who started the family store back in 1891 both died in the early 1930s. Both had sons who worked in the business and continued to run the store after they both passed. My father was one of the sons.

Back in 1900 the original brothers had wished to expand the business but lacked the funds to do so. Fortunately, both had cousins from the old country in Illinois who had established other nearby successful retail stores: one in Oregon, Illinois, and the other in DeKalb, Illinois. The brothers contacted the cousin in Oregon, which was about 10 miles from Dixon, about getting funds to loan them the money to build a new store. This cousin owned a men's store and didn't want nearby competition so an agreement was struck wherein the new store would sell only women's wear.

By 1969 we had moved the store a second time, and this new store—built in 1943—was the finest designed retail store in Dixon having some 12,000 square feet of selling space (see Figures 3.1 and 3.2). It not only sold women's wear but giftware, women's accessories, sewing supplies including fabrics, draperies, and other miscellaneous items. When my family and I moved back to Dixon, my cousin was still in the business. About 10 months later, just as I was getting adjusted to taking over the buying of women's wear, my cousin went into the hospital for a minor operation and died the day he went home. By that time I had convinced my brother, who was still doing scientific applications programming in

Chicago, to return to Dixon to help me in the store. Here we were at the end of January, 1970—two computer guys with very limited experience in retailing.

Figure 3.1: The front of our 3-floor store in Dixon. (SOURCE: Personal photograph.)

The business had about 40 people working in it who were entirely women, many of them quite elderly who had watched us grow up. Interestingly, the bookkeeper had worked for both of the previous generations of owners and was approaching 80 when we returned. She retired soon thereafter having completed a career of working continuously for the business for 61 years.

3.1 New retailer in town

Many people in Dixon told us they were glad to see some new, younger blood back in town. I adapted rather rapidly to my new occupation as a merchant and finally got the chance to really be in management. My brother and I made some long overdue updates to the business, and for the first couple of years things went well and business increased. Since the store was essentially a family business, there were a number of close relatives who owned a percentage, and my brother and I decided to buy them out. This was a bad decision, but then again one lives and learns through experience.

Figure 3.2: A small portion (about 25%) of the first floor of our store in Dixon. (SOURCE: Personal photograph.)

As the saying goes, all good things must come to an end. In the early 1970s the country encountered a recession that was felt by all businesses in town. To add insult to injury, in Sterling, Illinois, a town about 10 miles to the west of Dixon, a major department store built a new store that was similar to a Dillard store today. They had deep pockets, and we were financially stretched thin from buying out the other stockholders.

Now it was becoming obvious to us that our father's original wishes not to have us come into the store rang true. Age brings wisdom. We managed to hang on for a few more years, but the competition was getting fierce. At Christmas time few cars were parked in a large nearby parking lot, and customers got scarce. In the winter of 1974 the burden became too much for my bother, and he gave up the ship and left the business thus leaving me to dig out of the business problems by myself. I closed the store in mid-1975. That was an in-depth learning experience in itself for me.

3.2 The good and the bad

My time in Dixon was not a complete loss. True, I did lose a lot of money, but I gained some valuable experience. Being a young new member of the community, I was called upon to do a lot of civic activities. I headed Dixon's United Fund and brought in the highest amount of funds they had ever experienced. Then I was asked to head the county's Cancer Society and again brought in records amounts of contributions. I was even asked to set up a Red Cross county-wide blood program and was quite successful at doing that.

In addition, I joined the local Elks Club and the Freemasons and eventually became a member of the Shriners (which I still am today). One of my hardest tasks was to whittle down the store's staff. I say it was difficult because some of the women, now getting quite elderly, had been in the store for their whole lives. It was like firing your grandmother. They did not realize that we tried to keep them on using our own money because we felt sorry for them as we would for a family member. I made a number of mistakes simply because of my inexperience. In the end our good intentions were our downfall.

3.3 Computer activities in Dixon

My interest in computers was as strong as ever. In the evenings to relax I would continue to study new advances in computers, particularly supercomputers. Cray introduced his Cray-1 machine, and I got the instruction manuals for that machine and delved into his unique computer architecture. It was a 64-bit word length machine with single instructions being able to, for example, multiply a block of 64 words by another block of 64 words producing a block of 64 results. Wow! What a system.

I also started dabbling in hardware design because I wanted to see if I could logically design ultra fast hardware components. I had no access to any computers but had a pencil and paper and could practice my skills.

One other related activity was designing complex indexed file systems. My experience at Boise had developed a keen interest in new advanced file systems. In the back of my mind I couldn't get over the concept of attempting to produce a file system capable of emulating how the brain stored and retrieved data. I filled sheets and sheets with design details of extremely complex file schemes.

At that time, new lower-cost process-control computers were being introduced. Transistors were ubiquitous in these smaller machines. The term *mainframe* was gradually giving way to the term *minicomputer* to apply to these new machines. With computers—providing they had basic machine language instructions like arithmetic, comparison, and testing to alter program flow—one could do logic applications to emulate more powerful instruction normally performed in hardware. Logic is logic. For example, if a machine did not have an instruction to multiple two numbers containing decimals, one could always make a program that would do such complex functions.

An old high school personal friend Ed Lawton and I even tried to see if we could set up a small computer service bureau using a minicomputer and my computer knowledge. We thought that we might be able to service some small farm-town banks to do their check processing. That idea fell through for two reasons. First, we could not arrange the financing for such a venture. Second, most of the banks were run by older people who were suspicious of these new fangled devices.

3.4 Back to seeking greener pastures

I wound up my merchant activities in July of 1975. Once again I was looking for a new computer related position. I made a couple of trips to Chicago to talk to job search firms. The result I usually got was that I had been away from computers for nearly 6 years and my skills had *surely* degraded in that time period. I was getting nowhere in my search.

Then one want ad caught my attention. There was a company named

Telemed in Hoffman Estates about 30 miles northwest of Chicago near Elgin, Illinois, that was looking for a programmer to help design a 10 gigabyte—a gigabyte is one billion bytes—storage system for a new computer system they were getting. At Boise we were in the megabyte—one million bytes—range so the size of the system Telemed was talking about was a thousand times bigger. This sounded right up my alley. I called and made an appointment to visit them. I told them about my earlier experience with both programming in assembly language and designing the unique file system I did at Boise. I walked away from the interview with a new job in hand.

In closing our store in Dixon, I have only one regret when I think back to my days as a merchant. Julie, our youngest daughter, followed her interest and received a degree in Textile and Apparel Management with an emphasis in Marketing. Now she is the only Eichler left carrying on the noble profession of merchant. I wish now we still had the store for her to go into for I feel sure she could had made it a very successful operation. I'm sure that her grandfather and great grandfather would have been very proud of her as I am. She has that necessary marketing master "touch."

4

Telemed Days

Telemed's business was computerized processing of electrocardiograms (ECGs)[1], and they were good at it. An electrocardiogram is a medical test for detecting heart problems. At their Hoffman Estates headquarters they had a dual system each having two mainframes, a Sigma 7 to acquire transmitted ECGs via the telephone network, and a Digital Equipment Corporation PDPsystem10 to do the processing of it. Each year they processed over one and a half million ECGs sent in by doctor's offices, clinics, and hospitals. They were, by far, the world's leader in the field. Their staff not only had medical application programmers but even cardiologists on board. It was quite an operation as is, but they realized the field of computerized ECG processing was evolving.

Several competitors had introduced minicomputer systems that could be sold to larger hospitals—those that did 40 or 50 thousand ECGs a year—and Telemed could feel the pinch to their service. They needed to get into the minicomputer processing of ECGs, but all their people had experience on were mainframes where they used FORTRAN. This was a new ballgame for them. They needed a good systems programmer that could help them produce a new product.

Telemed was a successful business with plenty of cash. They hunted around and found a small company named Metromation in Princeton, New Jersey, who was developing such a minicomputer system that they could purchase, enhance, and sell to hospitals and other smaller ECG processing operations. But to do this they needed one or two program-

---

[1] Electrocardiograms are sometime referred to as EKGs since the German spelling of cardiogram begins with a 'K'.

mers to travel to Princeton and stay for a few months to get to know the new system which was in its final stages of development.

4.1 Hello Interdata

Interestingly, IBM had a researcher named Ray Bonner who developed an ECG processing program to be run on their System 360 mainframes.[2] This program was different from the home-developed ECG program that Telemed had been using. Metromation rented the program from IBM and used it as the basis of the new system they were creating. Metromation had searched for a minicomputer that was quite similar to the IBM 360 and found one manufactured by a company named Interdata also out of New Jersey.

Interdata had designed their computer to be a much lower cost alternative to the IBM 360 systems that companies could buy rather than rent from IBM. No one, to the best of my knowledge, at Telemed had worked on the 360 especially in machine language. Apparently I was a natural for the job I was hired for. They loved the fact that I was an assembly language programmer and knew FORTRAN as well.

So I moved the family to Elgin which was a few miles from Hoffman Estates and an easy 10 minute drive. Almost immediately I left for Princeton, New Jersey, for 4 months so I could get familiar with the details of the new machine. Accompanying me was a newly hired scientific programmer who had a PhD in aerodynamics engineering. His job was to concentrate on the FORTRAN portion of the ECG program, while mine was to concentrate on the rest of the system. I had really lucked out. Not only could I get my hands on a new minicomputer that I knew immediately how to program, but I also could work on large database design for the system.

Telemed's overall plan was to not only get a minicomputer they could immediately sell but additionally to develop a new database oriented system to store ECGs on utilizing newly developed massive disk drives that were being introduced. The Control Data Corporation was just coming out with a disk drive that could store 300 MB of data. Today we measure large memory systems in not only megabytes but in gigabytes

---

[2]Actually Ray had originally developed is ECG analysis program for earlier IBM machines and it was later migrated to the 360/370 machines.

and larger. A whole third of a megabyte was considered huge in those days. My duties were to primarily be involved with the creation of a database for these new drives.

4.2 A simplified explanation of ECG analysis

Before proceeding too far into this chapter I'd like to outline the general information flow through a computer to yield a medical analysis that is useful to a doctor. Back in the 1970s the transmission of digital data over public telephone lines was just in its infancy. We would consider fast a transmission over the telephone network of only 300 bits—about 25-30 bytes, i.e., characters, per second—quite state-of-the-art back then. Today at my house as I write this, I have a new fiber optic internet connection which transmits about 380,000,000 bits per second which is very roughly 38 million bytes per second and, if I wish I can up that speed by a factor of three for a few more bucks per month. We were literally in the stone age of communications in 1975 when I joined Telemed.

Fortunately, 25 characters per second was considered quite reasonable when sending printed material to a remote printer, more than sufficient for that purpose. But that's all we had to work with. Keep that in mind when reading the rest of this chapter. With today's digital data, it's a cinch to send data between two remote locations at very high speeds which obsoletes everything we did in those days.

4.2.1 How the heart works

The muscle contractions of the heart are kicked off by the conduction of a very weak electrical signal sent through the heart many times per minute. A rough analogy is how a single circular wave is propagated outward when we throw a stone in a pond. By throwing one stone after another rapidly we generate a series of waves moving outward. Although the electrical signal in the heart is very small, it may be easily detected on the surface of the body by attaching electrodes and having appropriate electronics to pick up these electrical signals.

With a normal healthy heart, the signal produced looks periodic in nature. If, however, there is a defect in ones heart—like a dead section of heart muscle—this changes the shape of this wave. It is the same as if a stick or stone stuck up through a section of our pond in the example above. The wave would be disrupted and no longer be circular. Depending on where the defect is on the heart, a highly trained heart doctor—referred to as a cardiologist—can see what is wrong with a heart. But, as it turns out, cardiologists don't always agree. Extensive studies of the analyses of many cardiologists yielded a general set of criteria representing a consensus opinion that is useful.

Several different companies have developed computer programs incorporating these consensus opinions producing several different computer programs to analyze these ECGs. To ensure that a computer program does not produce a wrong analysis—a very critical step in the medical field—almost all ECGs must be "overread" by a cardiologist. I don't know how much a cardiologist today gets for the service but it used to be $35-$45 per ECG or thereabouts. This made it an attractive business for a cardiologist to provide this over-reading service. It was also useful for other doctors who were not cardiologists but would find an ECG necessary to help a patient.

4.2.2 The ECG cart

A machine is necessary to pick up the signals from the heart. Today, with the advent of modern electronics, such a machine can be made small enough to fit in the palm of a hand. Such a machine was called an ECG cart. Today most ECG carts also have a strip chart recorder to put out a paper copy of the heart's signals as the ECG is performed. But back then the carts were generally big, clunky devices. For a non-transmitting cart requiring only a local strip chart, transmission is not really needed thus reducing the size of the machine. But to transmit an ECG somewhere else, more electronics are required. This also meant that the cart must be connected to a physical phone line. In summary, all a transmitting ECG cart does is detect the electrical output waveform from a patient and then transmit that signal somewhere to be analyzed.

If you were to have an ECG taken you would notice that the doctor doesn't place only 2 electrodes to your body. The cardiologist wants to see your heart from a number of different angles. Hence, multiple electrodes are precisely positioned on your body. Different combinations of the signals from these electrodes produce different signals providing various views of the heart in action. The "standard" ECG commonly used is called a 12-lead ECG in which 12 different waveforms are presented.

4.2 A simplified explanation of ECG analysis

These are grouped into 4 groups of 3 signals in each group. This means that three different signals must be sent at the same time to the remote destination. Today this a trivial thing to do but in the 1960s and 1970s this was easier said than done.

Figure 4.1: A transmitting electrocardiogram (ECG) cart. (SOURCE: Old Telemed sales brochure for the MEPC ECG processing system.)

4.2.3 Transmission of the ECG signal

Two types of data must be transmitted with an ECG. First the cart must send identifying information about the patient. This was done using the same mechanism a phone uses when dialing a number, i.e., touchtones. In locations where the phone companies were more primitive, such as far out in the country in a small farm community, an alternative simulating rotary dialing was generally provided by the cart. Usually the cart sent this identifying information as a series of 20 numeric digits.

Transmission of the actual ECG data was much more complex as can be well imagined. To understand the clever technique used, one must understand the difference between AM and FM. Yes, it is similar conceptually to how AM radio stations are different than FM radio stations. An AM station sends out the signal by sending out an "amplitude modulated" signal. In other words, amplitude refers to the voltage of the signal being sent out. Just like there is a difference between 5 volts, 12 volts, and 120 volts, volts are a measure of the amplitude of a signal. A 120 volt system—such as the electric power coming into one's house—would certainly give one a powerful shock, whereas a 5 volt shock would not hurt anyone. (There are some other differences, but this is sufficient for our discussion here.) Sending data using a voltage varying, i.e., amplitude varying, signal proves to be quite error prone because of noise on the phone line and other technical factors. Think of how a thunderstorm produces much static when listening to an AM radio station. Besides, non-digital telephone transmission over copper wires is horrible for transmitting any type of amplitude modulated signals.

On the other hand, thunderstorms have practically little effect on a FM radio station. Rather than vary the amplitude of the signal, an FM modulated signal converts the voltage variations into frequency variations. Varying the frequency means varying time rather than amplitude, and phone circuits are quite efficient at carrying this type of signal. This can be done rather easily by electronic circuitry. So carts in those days contained the necessary electronics to convert the voltage varying signals from the body into a frequency varying signals. Using frequency varying signals work quite well for ECG transmission. If a standard was adapted to send each of the three signals between three different ranges of frequencies, these signals can be added together and sent simultaneously. In fact, whenever you use a touchtone dialing pad on a phone to send the number you are calling, two different tone frequencies are combined together for each digit dialed.

The net result is that telephone lines can transmit frequency quite accurately which is the reason you can usually recognize the voice of a person you are talking to on a phone call without much distortion. Hence, early on the problem of sending analog data—data that is voltage varying—over standard telephone lines was practical even though attempting to send digital data was extremely limited. But how about at the receiving end of the telephone connection? For this we need another electronic device called a *receiver*.

4.2.4 The ECG computer receiver

At the computer end of the telephone connection, the procedure was reversed. Initially, three "band pass" filters were employed. Each filter would only be able to pass a specified frequency band. The composite signal was then broken into the three different transmitted signals, one for each of the three ECG leads. The output from each of these filters is passed to an electronic circuity that converts frequency variations back into voltage variations, i.e., each frequency represents one voltage level. This, of course, is much easier said than done as I would find out much later.

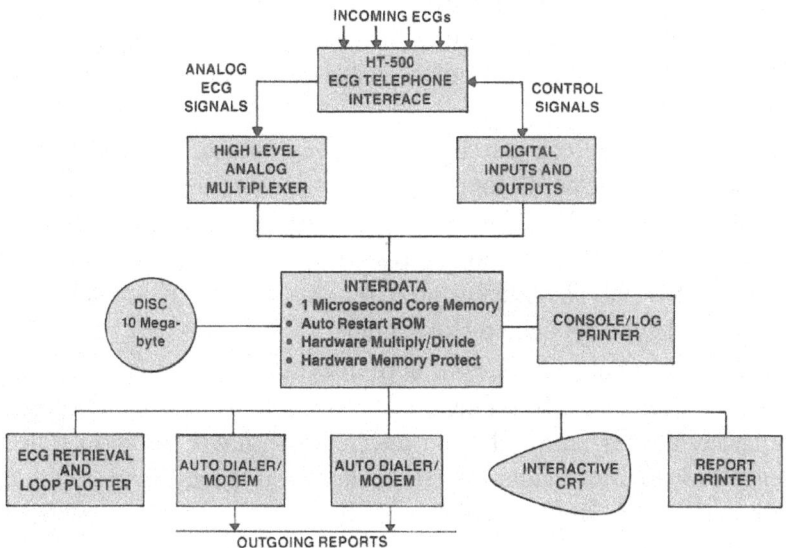

Figure 4.2: Typical components for an ECG analysis system. (SOURCE: Old Telemed 1976 sales brochure for the MEPC ECG processing system.)

One more step is needed before the ECG can be analyzed. The voltage levels must be converted in digital numeric values to be passed to the analysis computer. There are likewise electronic circuits to perform this function. So three voltage-to-digital converts are used, one for each of the three separate signals. Finally the data can be read into the computer. The device that performs all of the above steps is called an ECG receiver. This device is an extra electronics box that is connected to the computer. This is shown schematic form in Figure 4.2

4.2.5 Analysis and sending back the report

Once the computer has analyzed the ECG, it is necessary to send back the report to a printer at the facility where the ECG was produced. This could be done at a slow 25-30 characters per second as was discussed above. It is not that complicated to have a computer dial out on a phone line. The main problem that arises is that there were a wide variety of different printers on the market and each had its own idiosyncrasies. This too was something that caused me numerous headaches I was about to learn the hard way.

But what if the computer analysis was determined to be incorrect by the over-reading cardiologist? For this reason editing programs were also a feature of an ECG processing computer. The cardiologist would usually dictate the corrected analysis and then have someone in their office type it in via the editing program and initiate the transmission of the corrected report back to the sender.

So there you have it, the complete information steps through an ECG processing by computer. This was a much more sophisticated system than the relatively simple billing application that I worked on at Boise Cascade. Many more time-related tasks. One thing I had going for me was that the more modern computers had an "interval timer" built into the computer so I didn't have to do all the timing through convoluted programming like I had done on the UNIVAC. Whew... what a break!

4.3 Off to Princeton, New Jersey

Princeton was a nice town, small enough to get around in nicely but large enough to have good restaurants. Metromation's company was located northwest of town in a nondescript one-story. Downtown was where the famous Princeton University is located, and the college atmosphere was definitely present. The other scientific programmer and I rented an apartment on the east side of town where we could get to work in 10 minutes or so.

The Metromation people working on the project were quite friendly and consisted of a woman mathematician, a man who was a philosophy major but had gotten into programming in a way similar to how I did, and a very interesting fellow who had a PhD in applied logic and was, in my opinion, one of the finest systems programmers I have ever met. As the system programmer he was mainly concentrating on the realtime acquisition of ECG data, a very time-dependent process. The other two programmers were translating the IBM analysis program over to the Interdata.

IBM had written the analysis program for earlier machines than the 360 and so it was written in assembly language—the realtime acquisition portion—and Programming Language 1 (PL/1), an early IBM language they had developed that was similar, but more powerful, than FORTRAN.

Some time earlier Telemed had acquired a hardware manufacturer called Healthtech in Omaha, Nebraska, who made both ECG carts and receivers that could frontend the new minicomputer system. I can't remember if Metromation had acquired one of these receivers, but I'm rather sure they had since the new systems were duplicated and sold using Healthtech's receiver equipment.

There's not too much more to be said about my time in New Jersey except I managed to see some more of that area of the country when I was there. I got down to Philadelphia several times and found a fantastic restaurant where all the waiters were opera singers which was quite pleasant during fine dining. I would fly home about every other weekend to be with the family. When I was ready to drive home in the late winter, our son who was about 10 at the time, flew out and drove back with me which was enjoyable.

4.4 Back to Hoffman Estates, Illinois

The project was to have two separate, but interacting, parts. One was to get the computer up and processing ECGs. The other was to develop a mass storage system to attach to the analysis computer so that ECGs could be stored and retrieved. The PhD programmer I worked with in Princeton was assigned the first of these tasks, and I had to get the mass storage system up and running.

Telemed already had a buyer for their first one or two systems so they were anxious to get the systems ready to ship. One was to the Hospital at the University of Pennsylvania referred to as HUP. The other was to a cardiologist named Dr. Jim Wilson in Little Rock, Arkansas, who had a small service bureau that processed ECGs for St. Vincent Hospital in Little Rock and a number of doctors and clinics in Arkansas. Jim and I became good friends in years to come.

My boss was in charge of the overall project. One of the first things we had to do was hire some additional programmers to work with us. I put ads in both the Chicago and Minneapolis newspapers and was flooded with resumes. Since my experience with computers was quite extensive by that time, I loved to interview people for the job. I usually would play dumb just to see how much bullshit the potential hire would know and the actual depth of their knowledge.

I remember one fellow who had worked for Control Data Corporation in Minneapolis who I flew in for an interview. He had worked for CDC for seven years and appeared, from his resume, to be quite knowledgeable in computers. Playing dumb, I said that with one bit that I could represent either a 0 or 1, off or on. I then proceeded to "wonder" how many combinations could be represented by two bits. Appearing to be trying to figure it out, I wrote out all the combinations: off-off, off-on, on-off, and on-on, a total of 4 combinations. With apparent difficulty I turned on the problem of using 3 bits finally coming up with the 8 possible values. I then turned to him and asked him how many combinations could one represent with 8 bits, i.e., 1 byte. I knew the answer (2^8 which was 256). The poor guy seemed stumped. He finally ventured that the answer was 1x2x3x4x5x6x7x8 which was clearly wrong. With my previous experience I do know that anyone who didn't know that very simple relationship would not work out so I sent him home. Playing dumb really seems to work wonders when interviewing applicants.

Another applicant was a young computer enthusiast. Back in the days at Boise I had poured through the coding of the DOS operating system. In multitasking operating systems, one critical task is switching between the tasks to be executed so the code to do this must be fast and efficient. I was puzzled when whoever programmed that logic only used three completely rarely used instructions to do the task. I took those 3 instructions home and on one Sunday afternoon spent maybe five hours plowing through the logic used until I understood what he was doing. It was extremely simple but quite non-obvious because of how it was done. This young applicant and I got talking and he, to my surprise, had done some work on a 360 DOS system. Out of the clear blue he asked me if I had even looked at the task scheduling logic DOS used. I said yes, and he outlined the procedure to me. This was the type of guy I could really use. Unfortunately, one of the Vice Presidents of Telemed said we couldn't hire him because he didn't have a college degree. What a loss this was because the interviewee was clearly a brilliant programmer.

Anyway, I put together a super staff of four people: a PhD in electronics who had worked for General Motors, a mathematician who was an excellent scientific programmer, an applications programmer, and Brooke Boering, a man that put together, almost singlehandedly, a realtime computer system for one of Chicago's largest savings and loan bank.

During all this hiring, the PhD who had worked with me in Princeton hadn't hired a single individual preferring to do all the work on the analysis program himself. It finally got to the stage where this person left Telemed, and I, myself was tasked with hiring people for that area. I ended up with a staff of 8 highly qualified people who worked for me. Interestingly, I was the only one of the group that didn't have either a Bachelor or a Masters degree in computer science. In fact, I think they all had advanced degrees beyond a Bachelors. It was left to me to do all the systems programming work with the Interdata operating system.

4.5 Telemed's first MEPC customer

The first MEPC[3] system—not including the mass storage option—was to be sold to cardiologist Jim Wilson in Little Rock. It could be configured with two receivers or three remote editing stations. Our marketing department was filled with enthusiastic salesmen who knew zip about computers. This resulted in one over zealous salesman over sold Dr. Wilson's system with both two receivers and three remote editing stations. I would later have to educate the sales force on what they could and could not sell.

The computer was delivered and set up by some of our maintenance people. A short time later we received a phone call from them that the

---

[3] We pronounced MEPC like peps but with a 'm'.

system was not preforming like we said it would. This resulted in a threatened lawsuit in a heated exchange between us and Dr. Wilson. The discussion ended with one of our Vice Presidents offering to send me to Little Rock to see what I could do to fix the problem. The MEPC system had a 10 MB hard disk divided into a 5 MB fixed disk—which couldn't be removed—and one removable 5 MB drive (see Figure 4.6). I loaded up a removable disk with all the development software I needed and headed south to Little Rock. I was supposed to spend two days there but ended up spending ten.

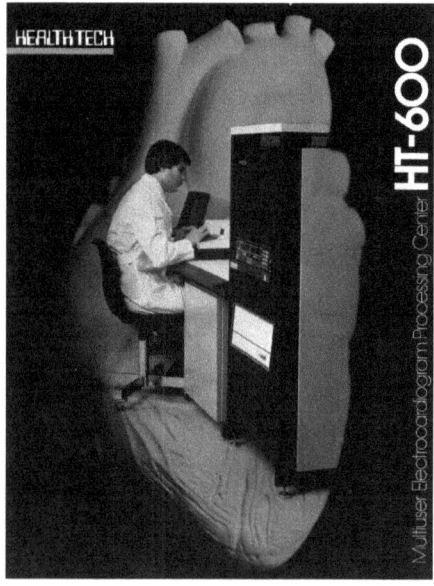

Figure 4.3: An electrocardiogram (ECG) cart. (SOURCE: Old Telemed 1976 sales brochure for the MEPC ECG processing system.)

Wilson's system had additional problems. His customers had a variety of different printers for printing out the computer's analysis. I first did some tricky programming to extend the number of remote editing stations from one to three. It was fun squeezing programs into tight spaces like I used to do on older more primitive computers like the UNIVAC.

I then turned my attention to the printer problem. This turned out to be a bigger problem than I had first imagined. Some printers required a two-way handshake between the computer, and the printer and others

4.5 Telemed's first MEPC customer

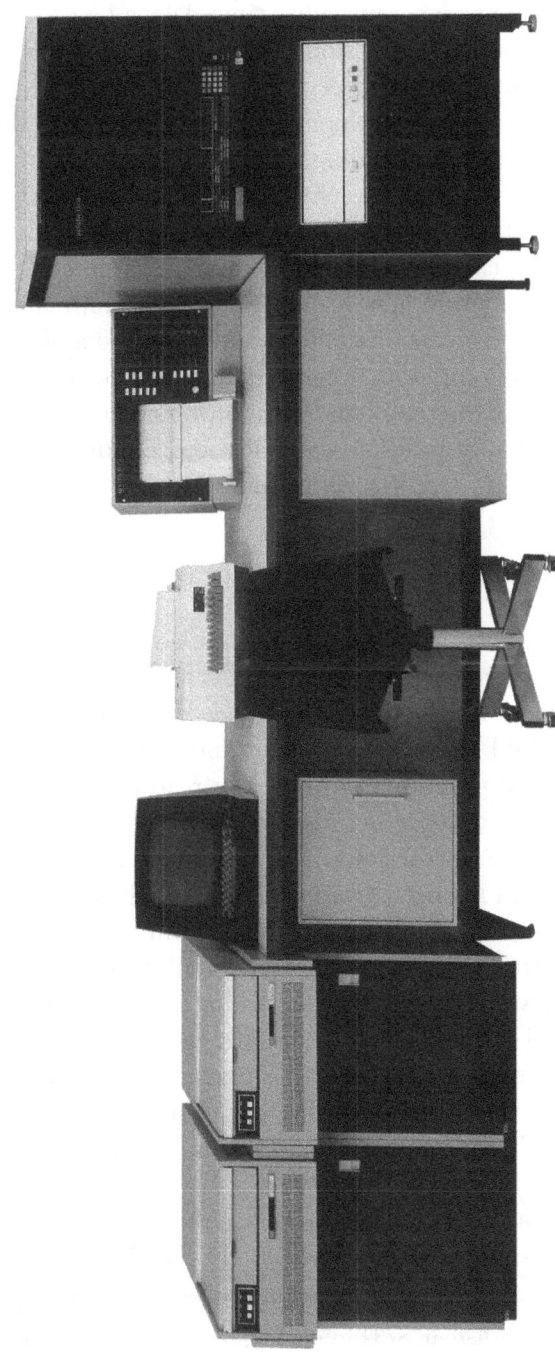

Figure 4.4: The MEPC electrocardiogram (ECG) processing system with mass-storage option. Shown from left to right are 2 high capacity CDC hard disk drives (these are not the 300 MB ones we later used for the EPIC system), operator station with keyboard and display, receiver(lower bay) with 3-channel direct writer above, and Interdata 7/16 computer.) (SOURCE: Old Telemed 1976 sales brochure for the MEPC ECG processing system.)

had special timing problems where varying time delays had to be introduced between steps in the transmission of data. I kept careful records on what changes were required so we could incorporate the changes in the new 7/32 system we were developing. Finally after the ten days were up, I had Wilson's system running like a well-oiled machine. During those ten days, I would explain each step of the process to the good doctor, and he realized that I had some expertise and knew what I was doing. He was a happy camper when I left. Our sales force later sold Wilson a 7/32 EPIC system. Whenever he travelled to Hoffman Estates his first priority was to see me as he felt I was the only one at Telemed who knew what was going on. I assume my trip to Little Rock to solve the problems with the MEPC really made an impression on him. I think he thought I could probably walk on water if the occasion arose. Later I would end up working for Dr. Wilson in Little Rock.

4.6 The Interdata 7/32

Interdata cut its teeth with a 16-bit machine called the 7/16. All the data pathways, i.e., *data busses*, in this machine transferred only 16 bits at a time, which, incidentally, held the cost of the machine down. Fortunately Interdata designed this machine using microprogramming which meant that small control programs were held in read-only memory (see Appendix C on page 165 for a further discussion of microprogramming). When a machine language instruction was encountered in a program, the machine executed a small microprogrammed code for that instruction to carry it out. Taking advantage of this microprogramming approach, Interdata soon changed this read-only memory to emulate a 32-bit machine using the same hardware as the 7/16 but looking to a programmer like it was a more powerful machine than it actually was.[4]

Telemed knew about the 7/32 machine and wanted us to transfer the analysis system to this newer machine in the next ECG processing system generation with the mass storage option we were developing. They ended up marketing the 7/16 systems under the name of *MEPC* for Multiuser Electrocardiogram Processing Center. The 7/32 systems were sold under the name of *EPIC* which stood for Electrocardiogram

---

[4]In the early 1980s Interdata actually introduced a true 32-bit computer called the 8/32. At a latter job I held I had an 8/32 to do development work on but that will be discussed in a later chapter.

4.7 My management style

Processing something or the other, I forget exactly what the last two names were. Perhaps, even, the name EPIC was just dreamed up by our marketing people. The 7/32 had a new and improved operating system which I had to make work with our ECG processing system.

Figure 4.5: The EPIC ECG processing system based on the Interdata 7/32 computer. This picture shows the 300 MB CDC disk drives used for the mass storage option. These drives used the disk pack shown in Figure 4.7. (SOURCE: Old Telemed sales brochure for the MEPC ECG processing system.)

4.7 My management style

Managing a staff of programmers is a unique challenge to say the least. Programmers are a breed different than many other occupations. They are usually smart and work independently. All they need is some general guidance and then it's up to them to do their tasks in the manner they see fit.

Back in Dixon when I was tasked with running the United Fund, Cancer Society, and Red Cross blood program, one of the secrets of my success was how I set up fund raising activities. I always made sure the field workers had achievable goal amounts. I never gave them impossible goals they couldn't meet. The result was that we brought in more funds and would break overall goals of the fund raising. And this worked beyond all expectations.

At Telemed I set up the goals and served only to coordinate activities. Every Tuesday morning I would hold a group meeting where I ensured that every issue related to system development would be solved by the group as a whole. I made it understood by everyone that this was a group project, and everyone had to buy into every decision we made. At these meetings I made a point that I was to be regarded not as the boss, but just as another programmer. If differing opinions arose, we would just continue arguing about the best way to proceed until everyone bought into our course of action. All decisions were joint ones, not ones dictated by their boss, i.e., me.

This went against the general management style by the other managers at Telemed who, for the most part, liked to dictate what had to be done. After all, isn't it the boss's job to direct their staff? I've never liked that kind of management myself. Many a time I've sat in on management meetings when the higher management would ask how long a particular project would take. Others would give estimates of maybe two or three months and then it would come to me, and I'd say it was a one-week project. I'd ask for my people to have two weeks as a little buffer in case we ran into problems. I gained the reputation around the place as being somewhat of a miracle worker, and I attribute that entirely to the quality of the staff I hired.

One challenge was to be able to coordinate my staff, most of who worked quite independently. I solved that problem by writing the overall control program—in assembler, naturally—and then defining, in detail, what all the interface formats were to be used between programs. In essence I was giving each programmer exactly what the input and output to his or her program would be. This technique worked exceedingly well for I could mock up data files so each person could work independently of all others. In fact, when all the component programs written over a period of months were ready and independently tested, it took less than a couple of hours and the entire system was working from ECG signal input to final report generation. In my personal opinion this shortness of integration time was remarkable to say the least. I attribute it to the fact that there was minimal interactions between the programmers.

I loved to put out challenges to my staff. We might have a heated discussion about how a particular task was to be done. I'd remind whomever suggested a particular approach of how hard it would be to do something the way they suggested and how failure was probable. Time and again whomever I was talking to would take on the challenge and work their fool head off to achieve success. Having a person setting their own goal is much more successful than assigning someone a specific way of doing something. They are challenging themselves so they know if they fail they only have themselves to blame. That is one of the main reasons my staff was so darn good. Everyone pulling for the same goal and everyone buying in to how we were going to get there. I should also mention that it has been my experience that most technical people who really enjoy their jobs—the kind of people I like to hire—are quite responsible and want to do their job well without much supervision. This is doubly true if they each feel they have a say in, and important part in, the overall project.

4.8 Yearly cardiology conventions

Every year there are two major conventions of cardiologists held in major cities in the south like Atlanta, New Orleans, Dallas, or Miami. Each November the American Heart Association (AHA) was held, and in March was the American College of Cardiology (ACC) was held. These conventions were where displays were set up in huge convention halls so manufacturers could demonstrate their latest equipment. Ten thousand or more doctors would converge on each convention.

At one of these shows held in Miami, Telemed was going to introduce their EPIC computer, and it was my job to ensure the introduction would be flawless. The company was spending close to $75 to $100 thousand dollars on their exhibit. My staff worked like hell day and night to get the system ready. I always worked longer hours than any one else to set a good example of the type of effort I expected from them. I remember working with three other guys most of the night. All of a sudden my boss showed up at 4:00 a.m. to see how things were going. He watched us as we would gather together to discuss our next step and then proceed to the computer to see if it would work as expected. Then we would gather together again and go through the same process, all the time joking and laughing between ourselves. My boss couldn't believe what he was seeing. He knew well that no other group at the company would work so hard and so many hours as we did and not be complaining like mad about the hours worked even in the middle of the night. By the way, the demonstration was highly successful at the convention, but I was like a basket case from lack of sleep so, after the system was up and running, Telemed put me up in a hotel in Miami for three days to just unwind.

4.9 Further comments on computer multitasking

Before proceeding, I think it is worthwhile to discuss something about multitasking on the Interdata and similar systems.

Multitasking computers take advantage of the vast difference between the timing of the different peripheral equipment attached to a computer. For example, it takes much longer to read and write data from or to an external device (printer, disk storage device, magnetic tape, etc.) which requires the program to have to wait until the operation is complete. Modern computer operating systems take advantage of this time difference through multitasking. Multitasking involves having many tasks running at the same time.

Well, not actually at the same instant. Most computers can only be executing a single program at a time. However, if it is determined that the executing program has to wait on a slower device, the operating system in essence pauses that program, and saves all the information required to resume its execution, and then passes control to another resident program that is ready to continue with its execution. A well written operating system takes care of this seamlessly. If, however, the operating system has some programming flaws, it is a nightmare trying to figure out what is going on. The closest analogy I can think of is that it is like juggling a couple of dozen balls at the same time. Conceptually the idea is easy, but implementation is a bear, especially for non-systems programmers.

4.10 Other reminiscences from Telemed

For example, the Interdata computer[5] had a multitasking operating system that was quite good at doing this juggling for slower applications, but when multiple time related things were going on that the computer had to keep up with—such as controlling time-dependent input—it had some real problems. Brooke, one of the programmers who worked in our group, had a very sophisticated application he was trying to implement. At the time we had someone from Interdata on loan to us who was one of the programmers who helped write Interdata's 32-bit operating system. With such high level help, finding a problem in the operating system would seem an easy task. However, this was far from the case.

Brooke was running into timing issues with his program and felt positive it was the operating system's fault. The systems programmer from Interdata said it was not the operating system causing the problem. There were some quite heated arguments going on with each person pointing the finger at the other.

I decided that I had to determine who was right since we needed an answer to continue development. I spent almost a week of time, both during the day and night, trying to figure out the source of the problem. Then one night around 4:00 a.m. I managed to isolate the problem. I could hardly wait until everyone came to work that day. It turned out Brooke was correct, the operating system screwed up. When I pointed to the spot in the operating system code that was in error, the guy from Interdata grabbed the programming listing of the operating system and immediately saw the problem. Whoever wrote that section of code had forgotten to set an important single bit on in one computer word that was essential. He called Interdata headquarters and had them correct the error in future releases of the operating system and thanked me for finding the error that was not supposed to exist.[6]

4.10 Other reminiscences from Telemed

At Telemed I had to be sort of a jack-of-all-trades which I enjoyed because there was never a dull day at work. A few things come to mind when

---

[5]The Interdata 16-bit 7/16 had one operating system while the Interdata 32-bit 7/32 and 8/32 had a different more powerful one.

[6]I developed a somewhat "rule of thumb" that I use to test systems. I overload them until they break. In realtime systems that is how testing should be done to provide the most robust system possible.

thinking back to those days. We sold a MEPC system to the Hospital at the University of Pennsylvania (HUP). After we got the system working flawlessly, the man in charge of the cardiology testing at HUP came to see it before it shipped to learn how to use it. He was a good guy and quite professional. We got him a cup of coffee which he placed on top of the computer. As we were standing talking to him, he accidentally hit the paper cup off the computer and right into the console keyboard typewriter toasting the whole unit. That turned out to be an expensive mistake because the device was selling for close to $2,000. Lesson: No drinks near a computer because accidents do happen.

Figure 4.6: 10 MB Pertec hard disk.(SOURCE: From a 1980 Pertec peripherals brochure.)

Figure 4.7: 300 MB CDC disk pack.(SOURCE: From a 1980 CDC Magnetic Media brochure.)

Our early systems all had 10 MB drives with a 5 MB fixed and a 5 MB removable platters similar to the drive shown in Figure 4.6.[7] Interdata provided a disk diagnostic program that was supposed to completely test the data integrity of these devices, but it was not foolproof. There were a small number of other manufacturers producing such drives. It was very frustrating to test a drive only to have it fail shortly thereafter at the customer's site. I was concentrating on the large CDC 300 MB drives (disk pack shown in Figure 4.7) and had many conversations with

---

[7]Prior to the coming of the personal computer based on microprocessor computer chips, the hardware for computers was quite massive. Disk drives like the Pertec unit shown in the figure were about 20 inches wide, 30 inches long, and weighed over 100 pounds. It usually took two of us to lift the drive and affix it to the sliding tracks so it could be easily pulled out for maintenance.

4.10 Other reminiscences from Telemed

the engineers at Control Data Corporation (CDC) who were exceeding helpful especially because these newer drives were just being introduced. This one senior design engineer told me that he thought disk drive development was nearing a limit because of how data bits were magnetically stored on the platter's surface. I often remember that when I see advertisements today for hand-sized drive holding trillions (terabytes) of bytes.

I was interested in how disk errors were handled by the equipment, so CDC gave me detailed data on error detection and correction procedures. This included a number of various worst-case bit patterns designed to test not only the disk platter surfaces but the electronics of the unit as well. When we started running into problems with the 10 MB drives, I wrote a small diagnostic program to use those bit patterns when testing these smaller drives.

I recall one instance where my program found half of our new drives had errors that the Interdata software did not find. Incidentally, I would run the same program on the 300 MB drives we used for development. At night before leaving work, I'd start my program running, and it would finish just before opening time the following day. Something else very interesting was that some of the bit patterns would work just fine on a disk pack while other patterns would find errors on the same portion of the platter.[8]

Our systems without the mass storage option used 10 MB drives. One of our customers called in and said their system was continually shutting down. We dispatched one of our guys to see if he could fix the problem. I spoke over the phone to him for several days trying to help him locate the problem with no success, so I hopped on a plane and headed to Dayton, Ohio.

When I got there this fellow was at his wits end. I decided the problem must be hardware oriented so I pulled out the drive—they roll out almost completely from the cabinet so the cover could be taken off, standard maintenance procedure—and I looked at the track detection mechanism. Data on disks are written in a series of circular concentric track patterns. To accomplish that, the read/write heads would use a

---

[8]With the 300 MB disk pack one must be very careful when putting a disk pack near the rear of the drive unit itself. These monster drive had extremely powerful magnets to move the read/write heads and sometime the magnet fields would destroy a track or two of data making the entire disk pack unreadable.

photo cell looking through a piece of glass maybe 3 inches long and 1 inch wide that had a series of lines etched on it, one for every disk track. I surmised that the problem was probably that the disk was getting mixed up finding the appropriate tracks. And sure enough, the glass was cloudy. I took a Q-tip soaked in alcohol and cleaned off the glass and the drive started behaving as it should. Problem fixed!

While we were developing the Telemed 7/32 EPIC system, we had our hands full and were in need of help. Management offered to pull someone else off a completely unrelated project and I said fine as long as the person had "driver" experience. A driver was a small software routine that enables the computer to access a particular attached device, in this case a specialized modem to dial an external printer—over a phone line— and transmit data to the printer. I was assured that the person was a very experienced programmer who knew how to accomplish the task.

However, a driver for a multitasking operating system was a task requiring some skill and knowledge how multitasking works in bloody detail. Since I was assured that the person assigned did know that, I gave him a copy of the notes I had carefully taken when in Little Rock for the 7/16 MEPC system. I knew the procedure would work because I had, by trial and error, found it to work. This was a critical link for returning the ECG reports. After a month the assigned person came to me and expressed that the task was beyond his ability so he was going back to his original group.

I again asked management for someone else, and they provided one of their top programmers to assist with the task. Another month passed, and we were fast approaching the delivery date for the system. This new man was obviously not acquainted with systems programming in multitasking operating system either, and he said the task was beyond his capabilities and left to return to his group. I think I've mentioned it before: good systems programmers are somewhat of a rare breed. They are hard to come by. Additionally, our system was required to acquire data in real time which put stress on the operating system. Most applications programmers just don't have the experience required for such systems where timing is a critical element. The same goes for many systems programmers. We even broke the Interdata operating system at one point because so much was going on at the same time. Luckily, I found the bug in the OS and fixed it. My experience at IITRI had taught me how to cope with timing issues. Good real time programmers

4.10 Other reminiscences from Telemed

are also hard to come by.

At this point I was getting somewhat frustrated so I asked one of my staff—a person with a Masters degree in operating systems—to do the task himself. I heard nothing from him as he worked except that he was having success. After several weeks passed and about a week before the system was to be shipped, he too came to me and said he was having problems like the others before him. He hadn't been able to even have the computer dial out on the phone line. Normally I'm a patient person because when working with computer systems, not having infinite patience is a severe drawback. This time I was really losing it. Here we had someone assigned to the task for over three months with still no results. I got upset and did a little shouting as to why no one had told me truthfully about the problems they were having.

It was a Friday afternoon, and the system was to ship the following week. I was supposed to attend a mandatory corporate meeting that afternoon. I skipped the meeting and decided this problem was critical and needed my attention immediately. I started checking the hardware and found that no one had even set the switches on the modem to their proper values. I wrote a few lines of programming to help me isolate where the problems existed. Within a hour I had the 7/32 not only dialing out but transmitting data over a phone line to a printer situated in the adjoining room. When my team member responsible for writing the driver returned from the meeting, I read him the riot act and unintentionally reduced him to tears. I told him that he had just wrecked my weekend plans and that now I had to write a driver that worked.

Over the weekend while I was busily working writing a workable driver myself, my man came into the building and into his office shutting the door behind him. By Monday he had succeeded in writing the driver code and announced to me that he had it working. I told him thanks and great work. The only problem, directly because of lack of understanding of the guts of the Interdata operating system, was when the computer dialed out and sent out the report, the entire system would stop processing until the report transmission was finished. This, of course, was not how it was supposed to work and would cause problems later, but I wanted to show him that I appreciated his efforts over the weekend. I put his driver code in this first system to be delivered. I'd have to come back later and do the driver the right way.

One other funny thing happened when I first started at Telemed.

We didn't have the Interdata computer in yet so I was using the DEC[9] PDPsystem10, one of the mainframes to type in coding. One of the programmers who had been with Telemed for a long time had written a program to do a game of "Star Trek." The player was Captain Kirk and he had to make decisions on what the Enterprise would do if attacked. I was well into the game—I normally don't play computer games—when it looked like no decision would be the proper one. I made the decision to blow up the Enterprise and suddenly all my files on the machine rolled up indicating they had been deleted. I was madder than hell only to find out later that this programmer had emulated the PDP10 deleting files. None was actually deleted. Needless to say, I was greatly relieved.

One of Telemed's systems was installed at a Hospital associated with the Hospital Corporation of America (HCA) in Nashville, Tennessee. The corporation owned hundreds of hospitals. I spent a couple of weeks bringing up that system but never got further than the room where the computer was located. A few years later when I was working for ECG Systems in Little Rock (see Chapter 6) I had the opportunity to once again visit HCA headquarters and met Dr. Thomas Frist Sr.—his son later became the U.S. senator from Tennessee—who was the President of HCA and took us on a tour of their headquarters. That was a major learning experience. HCA had a complete television studio that produced programs shown in each of their hospital rooms to patients.

One of the highlights of the tour was a small room containing one computer and one man. The elder Dr. Frist said he made more money from this room than any other place in HCA. Each night the person in the room would check where they could make the best interest rate on the hundreds of million dollars in their empire and transferred funds to that bank for the night. Now that was big money wisely invested making more money for the corporation. I found this fascinating to say the least.

4.11 Corporate politics

At neither IITRI nor Boise I did encounter corporate politics, or, if they existed I was not aware of them. My boss's boss was a Vice President of the company and was somewhat of a dictatorial person who believed

---

[9]DEC stands for Digital Equipment Corporation, a main manufacturer of computer.

4.11 Corporate politics

himself to be anointed by God himself. My boss did a quite successful job of ensuring my interactions with this person were minimal to his credit. He had worked for the company for three years and upon completion of this time he was supposed to get a sweetheart stock deal. I was in Little Rock working on that system when my boss reached the end of his third year. He called me to tell me he was quitting Telemed. Apparently three years of working for his boss was too much for anyone to long endure. At that time my job title was Group Leader. I now had to report to the Vice President which didn't please him since, in spite of my successes, didn't appreciate my management style. Yikes!

The first thing this guy did was to have me explain the minicomputer system to him. I thought this would be an easy task but it was anything but. I would say step one was this, step two was that, etc. He said I had to draw him flow diagrams rather than just talk about it. I don't think he could program his way out of a wet paper bag if his life depended on it. Then he proceeded to tell me that I was not management material and that I would never succeed at doing management work. Higher level management would just walk all over me because I was not prepared to be in such an environment. He then showed me his new organization chart, and I would then be reporting to another manager who likewise didn't know anything about our minicomputer system. This new manager was a nice guy but adhered to the philosophy that the boss had to direct his staff in every breath they took, i.e., micromanaging everything. I don't know why so many management people I've encountered feel such a deep need to behave as they think a boss should by micromanaging, but so many do expecting that is the way to get results.[10]

In short, I was getting tired of having to continually attend management meetings which not only didn't produce anything worthwhile but ended up slowing down the entire development effort. We had a critical system delivery schedule to meet an important goal for the corporation, and it was almost stalled to a dead stop. The Vice President offered me a senior position—he recognized my technical abilities—and wanted

---

[10]In part I suspect it might be that a great number of managers don't have the skill set of those they manage and therefore feel obligated to do something to show their worth. I've never assigned a task for someone that I wasn't able to do equally or better than the person assigned could. The trick is to hire dedicated people, motivate them to buy into the task at hand, and then stand out of the way while they do their thing. Micromanaging does exactly the opposite. Maybe that is why I've gotten good results over the years by minimizing micromanaging.

me to give up management. He even wrote up my job description, and before leaving on a month long vacation to Africa, left it on my desk and told me to put it in a want ad in both the Chicago and Minneapolis newspapers to find my replacement.

I took it to the Human Resource director and showed it to her. She showed it to the President of the company who immediately came back to my office and asked me if I wanted to give up my management activities. I said no. So he ripped up the sheet and said he would have a long talk with the Vice President when he returned.

The President then called my entire staff, one by one, into his office to find out their opinions. All of my staff knew about the difficulties I was having with this VP and he learned how loyal they were to me and how they enjoyed working with me and how progress had slowed as of late due to this VP. I told the President that I couldn't take any more of these goings on. He finally sought me out in the company library, and I told him that quite frankly, there was no way in hell that the system would be ready for shipment with this guy in charge and that the VP didn't know his ass from a hole in the ground. That was Tuesday. He asked me to be patient and that Thursday upon arriving at work I saw a company-wide memo from him saying the business was sorry to have the VP leave the company and wished him well on his future ventures. *Now who is the one not to know anything about playing corporate politics*, I thought to myself! To fill the VP vacancy they brought in a guy from Omaha who looked and sounded just like the movie actor Andy Devine.

The new VP was a likable person, and we ended up friends. The only problem was that I still reported to my new manager and that would continue. Also, the new VP said he wanted to cease new system product development and concentrate on maintenance instead. I was not in favor of this at all. I had finally reached the decision to leave the company. My new manager asked me to go to lunch with him and at lunch ordered some wine with the meal. As if it was planned—it was—I slowly fumbled with my wine glass looking down at it and said I would be leaving Telemed. This hit him like a hammer since I was needed to get this important new system for delivery to Orlando, Florida.

Upon our return to the office, he made a bee line to executive row. The company President was not there that day and so my manager took over the President's office and said he wanted to see me. He wanted to put on the appearance of a big-shot executive and had been authorized

4.11 Corporate politics

to offer me a $5,000 bonus to complete the system by a planned system delivery date. When I got to the President's office, I grabbed a secretarial chair and rolled it and sat on it just like a spoiled kid who was about to be reprimanded. There my manager was with his feet propped up on the President's desk to look important. He offered me some of the President's candy which I politely refused. He made me his new bonus option which I politely also refused. It appears I had thrown sand into the smooth corporate management gears.

One of the Healthtech engineers I did receiver development with in Omaha was a good friend of both mine and the new VP. He just happened to be at Hoffman Estates that day and when the new VP saw him he asked him into his office. The VP asked him, "Who is the Eichler character that is causing so much trouble". My friend said he would stop by and ask me what was going on which he did. I told him the whole lengthy story, and he immediately went back to see the new VP. He told the VP that it wasn't me who was screwed up but rather it was the rest of the corporation. The new VP asked him to arrange a dinner meeting with just the three of us attending that evening. He also made it clear that he didn't want my current manager to know anything about it. The 6:30 dinner meeting adjourned about 11:00 that evening. The new VP asked me to write out all of my wishes and that he would see that he would ensure they were fulfilled. The next morning I submitted a paper to him saying I wanted to have the title of manager, and I wanted to report directly to him among other things including a raise in salary. Later the new VP said the hardest demand I made was to take my group away from my current manager. To do this in a face-saving manner, he set up an advanced planning committee and appointed my manager to it so he would no longer have the time to be my direct boss.

Over the last few previous months, we had hired a contract programmer from a consulting business—Analysts International Corporation (AIC)—to help in our efforts on the new system. The fellow from AIC knew the problems I was having at Telmed and told his office manager about it. I met with his manager, and he wanted to know if I would consider working for him as a consultant as he was in the process of forming a new AIC office in the Chicago area and liked my background. I would meet each week with him and his staff and was brought up to date on new features of IBM's 370 line of computers which had replaced the 360 line. This time I really decided to leave Telmed for still greener pastures. By this time I realized that I enjoyed new product development; maintenance programming was just not in my DNA.

5

Analysts International Days

I became a consultant with Analysts International Corporation (AIC), a successful and respected "programmer for hire" firm that was started in Minneapolis, Minnesota. AIC had been formed by several programmers who had worked for major computer companies such as UNIVAC, Cray, Honeywell, CDC, and IBM. In those days Minneapolis was a hub of computer companies, and many of the popular computers were designed and manufactured there. Over a period of several years they had opened a number of offices[1] and now they planned on opening a new one in the Chicago area. The staff was small and I was considered a valuable addition to it based on my background experience. The office was located in Woodfield, Illinois, in the Woodfield Mall complex not that far from O'Hare airport and slightly east of Telemed.

The manager was young and energetic and had obtained a number of contracts, entirely commercial businesses from the Chicago area so that there was plenty of work to keep us busy. I remember three noteworthy projects I worked on there.

Shortly after I joined AIC, one of the Vice Presidents came to Chicago to meet all the new staff members. There were six or eight at the time. It was common those days for making slight "enhancements" on the resumes AIC used to promote their services or so it seemed to me. This was not done in an attempt to deceive clients but more to show that AIC had vast experience and resources which they had.

---

[1]Their offices were in Atlanta, Binghamton, Cleveland, Dallas, Denver, Detroit, Houston, Huntsville, Indianapolis, Kansas City, Los Angeles, Milwaukee, Minneapolis, New York City, Philadelphia, Portland, St. Louis,San Francisco, Seattle, and Spokane.

This VP took all of the staff out for beer and pizza one night, and while eating he asked the various employees about their computer expertise. When he came to me I mentioned the UNIVAC 1105, and he questioned whether that was real experience or did I just pad my resume a little. I believe the reason he questioned me was that he apparently had worked on an early UNIVAC since he was from the Minneapolis area. To show him I was not just pulling his leg, I asked him what the instruction with the op-code of 37 was. He said that was a return jump instruction. Then he asked me what an op-code of 61 was, and I replied an external function. I came back asking about the op-code of 45, and he said an unconditional jump. This went on for several minutes and then, with a very surprised look said, "By god, you did work on the UNIVAC 1105!" I found this whole episode quite amusing.

5.1 The hospital in trouble

The Michael Reese Hospital was located very close to IIT near Lake Michigan. Living in Elgin, I could take the Elgin-Chicago train—like a typical commuter—to the city and then though a combination of subway, elevated train, and bus to get to the place. Their problem was that practically all of their programmers had left en mass, and in the process had sabotaged a lot of their programs. I have no idea what had caused such an exodus but apparently working conditions were not the best when it came to programmers. Apparently this downward trend continued and in 2009 the hospital closed its door permanently.

They had an IBM 370, the successor to the 360 series. I believe their people used IBM's Report Program Generator Language (RPG), a very high level simplistic (at least to me) business oriented scheme to generate reports. It could be taught to untrained workers which was one of its main advantages. All one had to do was specify what the input record looks like—what card column does the field start and end in and what type of field is it like numeric or text, etc.—and then what the format of the output report designed in the same manner via fill in the blanks on a form. The RPG program will take that data and create a report. A bare minimum of real program logic was required on the part of the "programmer" if you use that term broadly. Fixing the hospital's problem was a no-brainer and easily accomplished.

The one thing I remember about that system was IBM's Remote Job

Entry (RJE) station. At IITRI, Boise, and Telemed, I could get actual time on the computer so I could quickly debug programs. It is true that at IITRI, when using the IBM 7094, I had to turn in decks of cards and contend with a batch-processing environment. With this newer RJE technique, a substation could be set up with a display, card reader, and printer so batch jobs could be submitted remotely saving one having to physically take cards to where the computer was located. I think that Michael Reese even set up a RJE station at somewhere in downtown Chicago where they had an office. This was still back in the days where to get a dedicated special phone line to establish a communications link and was cost prohibitive except for large organizations. The internet would not become available on any type of useful basis for another ten to fifteen years.

5.2 United 'X' Corporation and COBOL

The reason for the X in this section title is that I can't remember what the X stands for. Was it United Container, United Foods, or something else? It was a commercial business located in a high rise in downtown Chicago. Theirs was an IBM shop, and AIC was hired to provide a programmer to program some relatively simple commercial application for them.

When I walked in and talked to the man who was head of the programmers, he outlined the task for me and I said that it will just take me a few days to rustle something together for him. What I actually meant, but didn't say, was give me a day or two to learn COBOL to write the program. That was on a Thursday and so Friday morning I made a bee line for my all-time favorite bookstore—Kroch's and Brentano's on Wabash Street in Chicago—and bought a book on learning COBOL. I felt like I was one of the owners of K&B because of the large amounts of money I had spent there over the years. They had the finest collection of technical books on almost any subject one could imagine, and it was a favorite hangout of mine. Need information, head for K&B.

As I rode the train back to Elgin, I started reading though the book cursing all the way; I disliked the language so much because it was more like writing a book than writing a program. Anyway, that weekend I finished the book and wrote a 350 line program on paper that I typed into IBM cards Monday morning. I submitted the deck of cards to operations and got my results back that afternoon and it had one error, one misspelled word. I looked back at my papers on which I wrote the code and found out it was just a typo I had made on the keypunch machine. The client was very happy. That was the first time I did the COBOL thingy and luckily didn't have to (meaning *forced*) to do it again until much later.

5.3 Telemed as a client

I got a call from Telemed informing me that they had some work on the Interdata 7/32 operating system and wondered if they could employ me—through AIC of course—to do the work. They said it was only for a week or so. I talked to my new boss, and he arranged an official contract with Telemed for the job. While I was at Telemed, one Tuesday morning they informed me that they were having issues with their assembly of EPIC systems in Omaha. They had moved all of the manufacturing activities from Chicago to Omaha where they were manufacturing receivers and ECG carts. Telemed was wondering if I might fly to Omaha and give them some help with a work-stoppage issue they were having. I told them I could help, although I had to be back by Thursday evening. My son was in a sports event that evening, and I had promised to be there. So off I flew to the wilds of Nebraska.

I had only been to Omaha once before and that was to visit a hard disk manufacturing site of CDC which had been an interesting trip touring that facility. My friend at Healthtech—the same friend who arranged that extended dinner for me with the new Telemed VP months before—met me at the airport. When we got to Healthtech in the late afternoon, the first thing I did was to sit down at the 7/32 console and tried operating the system I had designed. It was like walking through a muddy field while duck hunting. The system was running slower than molasses in winter. I started trying to locate the source of the problem.

My friend told me he had contacted Interdata the day before, and Interdata was flying in two engineers to work on the problem, one from Oceanport, New Jersey, and the other from Kansas City. Both were expected to arrive before noon on Wednesday. Meanwhile I worked on and on.

Wednesday morning both men arrived, and I was kicked off the machine so the "experts" could diagnose the problem. I watched as the

5.3 Telemed as a client

pair worked and worked with no results. One of the guys was a cigarette smoker which was extremely unwise when around the large CDC 300 MB hard drives. With those drives the read/write heads literally flew above the surface of the rotating disks themselves at a distance from the surface measured in micro inches. It was literally the equivalent of flying a Boeing 747 full speed five feet above the ground. Smoke particles were many time larger than this extremely close distance of micro inches. And sure enough, they crashed one of the drives costing several thousands of dollars having to replace both the disk (shown in Figure 4.7 on page 78) and the multiple read/write heads. The engineers continued throughout the day and by Wednesday evening were still stumped as to what the problem was.

When I arrived Thursday morning, the two were still at it. I called my friend aside and informed him my plane home was due to leave in the early afternoon and that if he wanted the system fixed, to call those guys off and let me get my hands on the machine. This he did and within an hour and a half I had located the instruction that was causing the problem. Knowing a specific instruction that was causing the problem led to a specific portion of the hardware so the problem may be analyzed and corrected. Knowing as much about hardware design as I do now, I could have fixed the problem with a screwdriver to adjust one variable resistor, but I didn't have that advantage back then. I let the engineers back on the machine and took off for the airport. I later learned that the guys at Healthtech had mixed up different versions of the central processor unit's boards and that was the source of the problem. Interdata had changed their timings slightly enough to make a lethal combination that brought the machine to a near standstill.

A few weeks later I received an unexpected call from Arkansas; it was Dr. Wilson on the phone. He had purchased a new EPIC 7/32 system and when he asked what happened to me, Telemed wouldn't tell him. It took one of his office staff to track me down. I was one of the few people at Telemed that he considered to have his head screwed on right. He asked if I might take a trip down to Little Rock and talk about the new system which would shortly be delivered to him. He was clearly worried especially when he learned I had left. I said that I would be pleased to visit Little Rock again.

6

ECG Systems Days

When I arrived in Little Rock Dr. Wilson was waiting for me at the airport. He told me how pleased he was to see me again and off we headed to his facility by St. Vincent Hospital. Nothing much had changed since I was last there. We sat down for a long talk, and I saw all of the people there I had previously met. The doctor said I was to have dinner at his house that evening where we could talk at length.

After dinner we discussed his business and where he saw it going in the future. All of his curent systems used the IBM Bonner analysis program. The new 7/32 EPIC used the Telemed analysis program, and this bothered him. When I initially designed the EPIC system I designed it specifically to be able to run both the IBM Bonner and Telemed analysis programs depending on physician preference. After I left Telemed junked the idea of converting the IBM program for the system. I would later find myself testifying in court as an expert witness for a doctor in Indiana who bought the "works," an EPIC with the mass storage option. He specifically bought the system on the premise that it would run both analysis programs.

Wilson wanted to expand his service coverage and wondered if I might be interested in working for him to develop a new system. This would be the third ECG system that I would be heavily involved in the development of. Having a taste of working as a consultant for AIC, I realized that although it would be interesting, my primary interest in new product development was even more interesting and challenging. After a couple of months of discussion, I was offered a position as Technical Director at ECG Systems in Little Rock. Later I was promoted to Vice

President of Technical Development.

6.1 Moving to Little Rock

I moved to Little Rock at the beginning of November in 1978. I got an apartment and left my family until we could sell our house in Elgin and our three children finished school in the following spring. What I didn't anticipate was that the 1978-79 winter would be a killer in northern Illinois. That year we had a total of 110 inches of snow at our home, and all kinds of weather-related problems arose. On New Year's Day, over a foot of snow fell that I had to shovel out. Three for sale signs were buried in our front yard, and there were two six foot snow banks due to shoveling at the end of our driveway. Incidentally, Little Rock even experienced 11 inches of snow one day which was a near record amount. When spring finally sprung, we sold the house, and I moved the family to Little Rock.

6.2 The IBM Bonner analysis program

A group at Dalhousie University in Halifax, Nova Scotia, Canada, had converted the IBM program from PL/1 and assembler language entirely to FORTRAN. We could get the program from them and adapt it to an Interdata machine. To get my development effort off to a good start, ECG Systems bought an Interdata 8/32—a true 32-bit machine—for me at the cost of about $135,000. It had a magnetic tape drive and a 300 MB disk drive. The disk unit was a newer and smaller, rack-mounted unit—about the size of a 10 MB drive—that was fully enclosed so smoke wouldn't crash the drive. One fast and beautiful machine.

One nice feature of the Dalhousie software was that there was included a magnetic tape containing 350 sample ECGs that IBM provided them. This calibration data—along with detailed intermediate results—was provided to ensure that any conversions of the program could be checked on a bit-by-bit basis. IBM wanted any such conversions to be perfect. The Interdata 8/32 machine was to be delivered several months later so in the meanwhile Interdata provided us with similar machine in Dallas that I could do my work on. I made many trips to Dallas during that time period, most extending over several days. It was a debugging

6.2 The IBM Bonner analysis program

nightmare needless to say.

As a side note, I generally attended a conference each year on computerized ECG processing. I enjoyed these because I would meet and talk with others in the field including people from Telemed. Though computerized electrocardiography was sort of a specialized field, the attendees group was of reasonable size. During the days we would hold meetings, and in the evenings we'd have an extended cocktail hour where the informal talk was mainly technical. Every now and then Ray Bonner from IBM would attend, and when he did our conversations were quite interesting. He always wanted to know how I was doing with his program. Another frequent attendee was Dr. Gordon Dower from Canada. I got to know Dr. Dower quite well, and he even visited me in Little Rock once. His method of obtaining and analyzing ECGs was different than the conventional way and was used by NASA to monitor the heart signals of astronauts in space (and probably still is).

One time I was in Dallas and planned to fly back to Little Rock and then out to Monterey, California for one of those conferences. Unfortunately, Dallas experienced an ice storm of epic proportions, and I was stuck. Being from the "nawth" as southerners would say, I knew how to drive in snow and ice and got around fairly well. I got a kick out of the Texans who were really struggling. After several days I finally got out to the airport and asked if they had any flights to California, which they did, so I changed my ticket and headed for the land of sun. Now back to the more important topic at hand: ECG timings.

The FORTRAN sections of the program worked relatively well, and although data was coming out the other end, there were all kinds of problems I encountered. The IBM program consisted of some five or six programs that must be run in sequence. I thought it might be a good idea to see long each of the programs ran to millisecond—thousandth of a second—accuracy. What I found amazed me.

ECG analysis is broken mainly into two parts. The first part is when pattern-recognition of the ECG signal was done. The output of this part was a large group of measurements. The second part—and this was written in FORTRAN—was to apply ECG criteria to these measurements. It became immediately obvious to me why IBM had coded the pattern-recognition portion in machine language; it was extremely time consuming. The FORTRAN programs took about as long as it took to say the word FORTRAN. All the time was consumed by the pattern-recognition code. I then and there decided to take advantage of the Interdata machines' similarity to the IBM 360-370 computers. I would use assembly language for that part of the analysis. In the end I got this part running literally like a bat-out-of-hell while the ECG was being sent.

6.3 Introduction to hardware design

Once the analysis was running smoothly through all 350 test cases matching the results bit-by-bit, my attention turned to the receiver problem for our new system.[1] I decided that I would tackle building a receiver from scratch, i.e., designing all the electronic circuitry myself.

For years, I had been learning electronic design. In those days, when one bought an expensive minicomputer, the manufacturer would deliver a complete set of electronic schematics along with the machine. At Telemed I would dig through such schematics to understand more about the machine so I wasn't starting from ground zero. In fact, when in Dixon I had played around with some digital electronic design in my spare time. After all, logic is logic whether it is implemented in software or hardware.

The digital logic was pretty straight forward. Integrated circuit manufacturers provided an excellent source of applications examples to help them sell their products. If a design engineer needed detailed design information, the manufacturers provided it in bulk in tons of manuals. Eventually my collection of hardware manuals grew to well over 500. This was particularly useful when it came to analog circuits where my knowledge was the weakest.

When writing software I generally programmed and checked out one part before going on to the next part in the program. I figured that I could do the same with each hardware component I designed. That worked out quite nicely. My receiver (see Section 4.2.4 on page 65) required three bandpass filters to pull the incoming ECG signal apart

---

[1]Interdata's instruction set was very similar to the IBM 360. However, I found it handled some of the 360's instructions differently than the Interdata did. For example, the machines might round off numbers differently. The results would differ very slightly and finding the culprit really involved some heavy debugging, but it had to be done.

6.3 Introduction to hardware design

so I started there. Following filter design rules, I ended up with three beautiful filters that did the job quite well.

The next step was considerably more challenging. The output from each filter required that I had to convert the voltage levels to digital numbers so the analysis program could use them. This was accomplished using what is known as a "phase lock loop" (PLL). There were a considerable number of PLL designs that could be used to do this, but designing PLLs are more of an art rather than a science. All the components had to be tweaked over and over, and I was having limited success in getting one fast enough to lock onto the incoming signal. Since the ECG cart varied the output frequency of the signal rapidly, I needed a circuit to keep up with the incoming frequencies. I finally ran across a unique digital PLL circuit from National Semiconductor Corporation that worked like a champ. It would pick up a frequency shift in as little as one frequency cycle.

Once I had the circuitry working, my next task was to design a circuit board. I used large transparent sheets of clear plastic and would use red tape for traces on the top of the circuit board and blue traces for paths on the bottom of the circuit board. This was tedious, but it was a clever way to ensure that everything lined up properly. In later years there would be software I could purchase to do that design on a personal computer. I could send the finished plastic sheets away where they were photographed through either a red or blue filter. This was a standard technique back then, and it worked out quite well. I built a single circuit board for the circuitry for a channel and then made three of the same board, one for each of the three incoming channels. In all, I built a very reliable and exacting receiver for the project, but it took some time. I have an old saying that *"with computers nothing is simple,"* and this certainly was the case. Luckily, I had Jim Labahn, a co-worker, who was extremely good at reading ECGs and who could wield a soldering gun to help me in construction of the system.

One problem with complex electronic systems is proper calibration. A standard way of calibrating a piece of electronic circuitry is to use a known fixed input and then measure the output and adjust the components until it produces a known output. Most electronic technicians carry a boatload of equipment with them like signal generators and oscilloscopes. I figured there should be an easier way, namely building the calibration method into the product itself. Besides, I had to able to generate touch tone signals to be able to dial an outgoing number. Why not kill two birds with a novel approach?

To accomplish this I designed an unusual circuit that digitally generated three very precise frequencies under computer control. My final circuit generated three independent frequencies between zero and 4,000 cycles per second to an accuracy of one tenth of a cycle and then added these frequency together in the same way as an ECG cart might do. The neat part about this was that I could route this output back into the receiver so I could adjust things with an unbelievable accuracy with no external equipment required. Our system could literally calibrate itself, a real benefit if problems would arise. And I could use the same output circuit to dial a phone number.

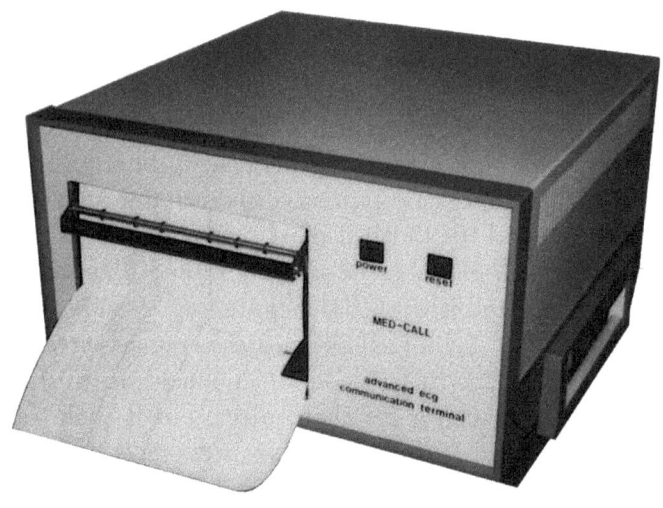

Figure 6.1: The ECG Systems "Med-Call" unit. (SOURCE: A personal photo.)

Another unanticipated advantage of being able to generate three precise independent frequency signals gave rise to a unique piece of equipment I dreamed up, designed, and built was our Med-Call device (as shown in Figure 6.1). We had a few of clients who wished to do over reads of ECGs at their remote location. To do this they needed to have the computer transmit a trace to their office. Recall that digital transmission was extremely slow, much too slow for the transmission of an entire ECG trace digitally. So I asked myself why not emulate an ECG cart and send the signal back using the same technique the cart does? Having my circuit that generates precise frequencies I could easily program the computer to re-encode the digital data in computer storage and send it back out as analog signals in the same manner as the cart originally sent it. So I designed a circuit using an Intel 16-bit microprocessor chip to control the Med-Call device. Finally I had something that none of our competitors came even close to having.

6.4 My secret ingredient

I wanted our new analysis system to be as simple as possible to operate. The best way to accomplish this feat was to write a unique multitasking operating system. The Interdata operating system was good but required learning how to interact with it. This was far too complicated for what I envisioned. At Telemed we used the Interdata 32-bit operating system and I found that it had confining bounds within which one must work. I needed a lean, mean machine, so I wrote an operating system for our new system. I included my hand-rolled database management system with an eye toward continuous unattended operation.

Power failure was a potential problem, so my database was designed to automatically fix itself should a power failure occur. After a loss of power event, once power was restored, our system was back to full operation in seconds without a human being involved. No lengthy reboot of an operating system thanks to the feature of core memory to retain its contents during loss of power. Also recall that core memory—with real core donuts—retain their content when a power fail happens. This meant that it was no longer necessary to completely reload the entire operating system which takes a lot of time.

But my real secret ingredient was that I could do most of the pattern recognition as ECG data were being received rather than wait until the entire ECG was acquired.[2] This could be achieved because my operat-

---

[2]The pattern recognition portion of the analysis consumed about 95% or more of the processing time. Being able to do this overlapping acquisition meant only less

ing system was under my full control. Both IBM and Hewlett Packard had similar minicomputer based systems they were marketing, but their systems took two to three minutes to run through the analysis before a report was sent back. With our system once the ECG was finished—it took about 22 seconds to get all the data from the ECG cart—all I had to do was run the very fast FORTAN programs which took about a second or two. While this was occurring I was already dialing the remote printer. Ours was, hands down, the fastest minicomputer ECG analysis minicomputer system in the world.

I always got a kick whenever we demoed our system at the cardiology conventions. Doctors would be amazed at the speed. What gave me even greater pleasure was when engineers from IBM and HP would try to get me to tell them was I was doing differently than they were. Incidentally, I knew many of these IBM and HP people from computerized electrocardiogram conferences I had attended. I silently gloated over that. I now think back to the sophistication of my operating system only to realize that it was developed at the same time as Microsoft was producing their non-multitasking DOS operating system for the personal computer. If I had a PC at that time, I could have produced a product that would have left Microsoft DOS in the dust! But I didn't, so dream on.

6.5 A few comments on core memory

In the mid 1970s, semiconductor memory chips began to appear on the market as a replacement to core memory. Of course, when the power would fail, they would all have to be loaded again with data since it would have been wiped clean. Also, early RAM chips were very low density, i.e., very few bits but this would change dramatically over the years. However, I believe it's interesting to say a few more words about core memory before leaving it in the dust. I started with core memory way back in the UNIVAC 1105 days, and the Interdata machines would be the last I would work on that utilized core.

In Figure 6.2 is shown some of the details of core memory technology. Each tiny core is just a small donut-shaped magnet that can change its polarity by the use of appropriate electrical currents passing through the wires passing through the core's center hole.

---

than 5% or so was left to do after the ECG was transmitted.

6.5 A few comments on core memory

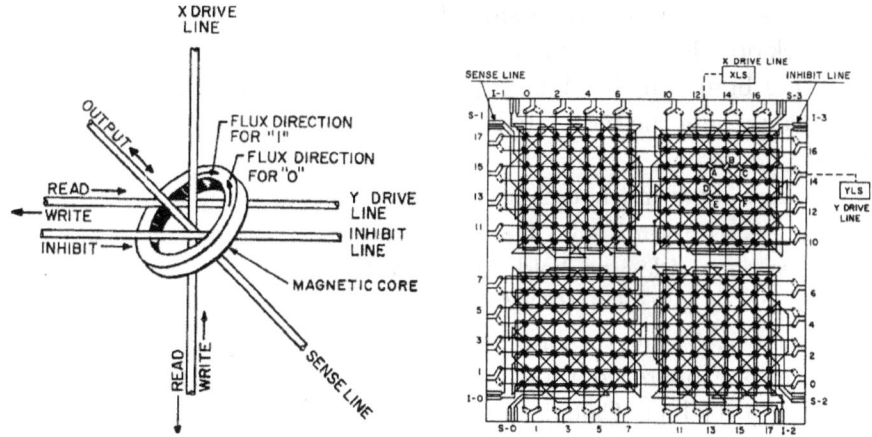

Figure 6.2: Core memory details. On the left is schematic of what a ferrite core looks like with the multiple wires running through it. Selectively passing currents through these wires the polarity of the core can be changed to represent either a zero or one. Each such core stores one bit. On the right is shown a small wired core memory containing 256 bits (32 bytes). (SOURCE: Personal photographs.)

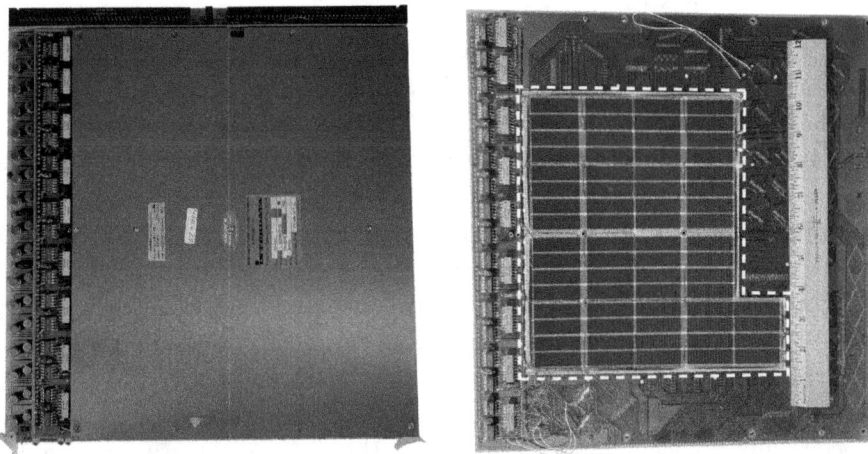

Figure 6.3: On the left is a 65,536-byte core memory board. It is about 16 inches on each side and about an inch thick. On the right shows the core array when the metal cover protecting the array is removed. (SOURCE: Personal photographs.)

Each core can store one bit of memory. The cores are threaded in a pattern as shown in the right side of the figure where each core is shown as a black dot. Figure 6.3 shows one of the Interdata core memory boards where the figure on the right side shows (outlined in white) the actual core array where the individual cores may be seen only when magnified greatly.

To show how much technology has changed, compare Figure 1.14 on page 18 to Figure 6.3. The array shown in Figure 1.14 was about 10 inches on a side and held 4,096 words of storage. Assuming each UNIVAC word contained 37 bits (36 bits plus one parity bit), that would represent 151,552 bits total in the module (the 1105 had 2 such modules). The Interdata board contains 65,536 bytes with 9 bits per byte (8 bits plus one parity bit). Calculating this out, the Interdata board contains 589,824 bits total. This means that the single Interdata board contains almost 4 times as much memory as the UNIVAC module did. But core memory was expensive. If I remember correctly, the Interdata board cost about $3,500. Today one can buy a million bit RAM memory chip for only a few dollars. How times have changed!

6.6 Remote changes to our system

Another interesting original innovation I did with our new system was to attempt to make a change in the software remotely. I reasoned that since we had the ability to do remote ECG report editing, why not use this feature to incorporate the same remote editing hardware—a terminal and a modem—to make a remote modification of the software using a terminal in Little Rock to call into a remote ECG system to look at portions of the disk contents and change them. Since I had listings of the operating system and the various programs and knew where they were located on the disk itself, patching the system was almost trivial.[3]

I wrote a small program called "Prober" that I incorporated into the system. I could remotely link up with it and made it so I could specify any physical 256-byte sector on the disk—disks are organized in blocks called sectors—so I could see the contents of each byte in the

---

[3] When I wrote the software for handling the organization of data on the disk, to make the system as fast as possible I had fixed positions for everything especially all the programs used. This was not like most file systems today that are much more extensive and more general purpose. As with the Boise suspense file, my file systems were design for limited flexibility and maximin speed and simplicity.

sector in hexadecimal and change them to effective patch the program. This worked out very nicely and saved air fare and a trip to where the system was located. Today such a technique of remote troubleshooting is common place, but this was decades before anyone else used it to the best of my knowledge. And the communications link to the computer was at only 1,200 bits per second: extremely slow in comparison to today's blazing communications speeds. I was, and still am, extremely proud of Prober.

6.7 A weird trip to New Jersey

ECG processing roughly falls in the bailiwick of medical devices. In fact, the drug giant Becton Dickinson bought out Telemed about the time I left. There was another drug giant—I forget the name—in New Jersey who had likewise decided to get into the ECG processing business, had purchased or developed a system of their own, but then wanted out.

My boss heard that they had two DEC PDP-11 based 16-bit systems they wanted to sell so off I went to New Jersey, once again, to evaluate these systems. They assigned one of their technicians to prepare them to show me. Apparently all their original computer programming staff had left since they were going out of the business, and this guy was the only one left. I watched as he worked on the machines getting them ready.

He apparently, hearing I was from Arkansas, thought we were from some "Podunk Junction" and didn't know much about computers. So as he was getting the systems ready he kept telling me that he has this strange power to put curses on people that didn't do as he wished. I've met a lot of weird people over the years and thought he was just a kook or something. He was inferring that if I didn't approve of the purchase that he would cast some sort of spell on me. I ignored his rantings.

He finally got done with putting together the machines and told me they were all ready to be shipped to Arkansas. I said, "Not so fast!" and told him that they had to process some ECGs before I got back to my boss telling him to consider buying them. Reluctantly, he said alright and proceeded to power the systems up. When powered up, sparks flew from them, and smoke started to come out. I laughed to myself and headed to the airport to catch a flight home.

In a certain respect, I wished that we had acquired one of their systems. When I was in Dixon and trying to understand hardware design, I had a set of DEC PDP-11 manuals and spent hours trying to work backwards determining what type hardware I would design to incorporate such an instruction set in hardware. To actually have one of those DEC computers at ECG Systems that I could play with would have been an additional learning experience for me.

6.8 Trouble was lurking in the wings

When Dr. Wilson hired me, he was working with a business consultant from Atlanta, This guy had grandiose ideas about greatly expanding Wilson's business, far too grandiose it turned out. They hired a business man from New York to head up the operation and a medical salesman from Atlanta to accomplish the expansion, and these fellows really knew how to spend money to excess. This resulted in a large outflow of money like it was water and before it became obvious, Dr. Wilson finances were being stretched to their breaking point. Wilson tried to get additional funding but was unable to do so. He finally found a buyer for the business, a successful businessman, Don Wyatt, from Mobile, Alabama, who had extensive dealings with a number of hospitals throughout the south.

The business did expand but this was just about the time when ECG carts were being built with microprocessors programmed to do the analysis within the cart rather than an external computer system. We put one system at ECG Systems main office in Mobile and another at Baptist Hospital in Pensacola, Florida. I have nothing bad to say about either Jim Wilson or Don Wyatt; better bosses I could not have asked for. After a few years, Don pulled the plug on the Little Rock office, and I found myself unemployed. In later years I would meet with Don Wyatt informally and still remained a friend until his death years later at the grand age of 87. Incidentally, I was still called upon to assist whenever our system ran into problems, but technology was changing the whole landscape of ECG processing.

7

Gunn Systems Days

For the first time in my life I had to avail myself and receive unemployment insurance. To continue receiving funds I had to demonstrate that I was looking for a new position. I finally came across a small company that was in the floor covering business—well, sort of. I never knew the entire history of the business, but from what I could gather—and this might not be completely accurate—the owner's father had a business selling floor covering in Little Rock. After the Korean War, his son, my new boss, returned home from serving in the military as an explosives expert. The son went into the business but realized, with the advent of the personal computer, there was a greater opportunity selling software for the floor covering industry than selling floor coverings themselves. Apparently when the father retired or died, the son sold or closed the business and started a business of selling software.

I told him of my experience in both hardware and software so he hired me to design and make a device to control the large machines that sellers of floor covering use to measure and cut carpet. He also wanted me to get to know a new 16-bit operating system he was buying from a software company in Walnut Creek, California. I don't remember all the details, but he thought this operating system was superior to Microsoft DOS for his purposes.

His business operated out of an old two-story house in a well established section of Little Rock not far from my home. It was an ideal location for me but the business, and particularly when it came to the owner, was the most unusual place I ever worked for several reasons. On the building's top floor there were three other programmers all of whom smoked like mad. While working there I suffered a heart blockage and underwent emergency bypass surgery. I probably would have died within days had I not known one of the cardiologists I worked with at ECG Systems. I also underwent a cervical fusion operation to fix a ruptured disk in my neck and had to wear a neck brace for several months. All in all, I had more medical problems at that job than any other I had ever held.

My boss thought he knew more about computers than he actually did. He had many conceptual views about different pieces of computer equipment that were flat out wrong, and trying to tell him what was indeed happening was like talking to a brick wall much of the time. In addition, something we—the other employees and I—didn't know until years after working there was that he never paid the business's share of funds into Social Security. That caused some hassle with the Social Security Administration people when I eventually retired. Luckily I had kept all of my earnings statements so I sent copies to the Social Security office and subsequently got credit for what was coming to me.

Another time when I got to work on a Monday morning, the empty room next to where my desk was located was filled with what I would estimate to be 200-300 shotguns. I later learned he also operated an antique business. Also he had no sense of privacy I could see. When I worked for myself in Dixon I was always cognizant of my employee's privacy and always ensured that all salary amounts were considered quite private, i.e., I would never let one employee know what another employee made. All other companies I worked for felt the same which I appreciated. However, at Gunn Systems on pay days he would write out a pay check and then just set the check upside-down on our chair whether you were there or not so anyone could come around and pick it up to see what the others were paid. I was never curious about others' pay, but I wasn't sure my co-workers felt the same as I did. This seemed to be somewhat disrespectful of his employees to me. This owner was unique.

7.1 The carpet unroller

Carpet comes to a dealer in a roll some 12 feet or so long and maybe 4 feet or more in diameter. They are really big and bulky to move around, so there is specialized machinery like a forklift with a long steel pole sticking out like a unicorn's horn. The pole is run lengthwise through the roll of carpet and it is lifted onto a large table perhaps 12 feet by 12

7.1 The carpet unroller

feet in size. There it is unrolled to the length needed and cut. Needless to say it is difficult to handle goods of that size.

My job was to design and develop a circuit board filled with electronics to attempt to automate the process. I based my design around a Zilog Z-8000 16-bit microprocessor, a popular chip at the time and cheap. Having only a 16-bit bit chip to work with was a hassle since programming this type of application in assembly language presented a challenge. Designing the basic computer hardware was not a problem. The problem came with all the other things the unit had to do.

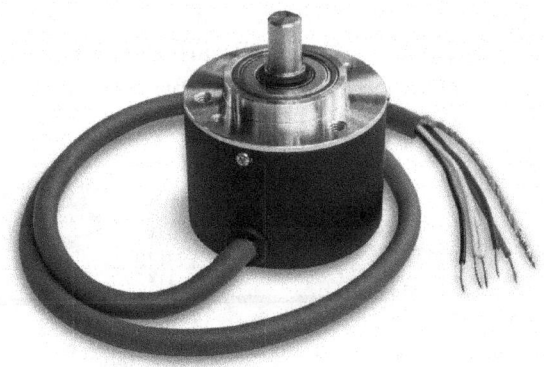

Figure 7.1: A rotary shaft encoder. (SOURCE: Original source unknown.)

The first thing the unit had to detect was the length of the unrolled material. I had to turn the motors on and off via my circuit as well as measure the material. I ended up using a small rubber roller a few inches in diameter attached to a rotary shaft encoder. This was a neat device as shown in Figure 7.1. It was essentially an enclosed marked disk that rotated on a shaft that we attached to a rubber roller. The disk was printed (or engraved) with tiny lines similar to how I described the track location mechanism on a disk drive. However, in this case the lines were not linear but rather circular around the outer portion of the disk. Also the unit had a small LED light and a photosensor. So when the rubber roller turns, it turns the disk and the photosensor picks up the rotation as the line whizzes past it. That way I could determine how much carpet material was unrolling. Naturally with such heavy carpet material, the roll of carpet picked up considerable momentum as the carpet unrolled so I had to slow the machine prior to it reaching the desired length and then move it slowly thereafter. Since there was no software for this device I had to write it myself.

Next my boss said the unit should be able to read a barcode on the ticket attached to the roll of carpeting and print out a new barcoded ticket to be attached to the remaining material showing how many feet were left on the roll. As soon as I finished one part of the design, he would come up with another function the unit should do which was somewhat of a pain. The reading part was simple. Hewlett Packard made a barcode reading wand that could pass the information from the barcode to the Z-8000 microprocessor. The fun part, I say that somewhat sarcastically, was that I had to print out a new barcode on an old dot-matrix printer. Of course there was no ready-made software the the Z-8000 to do any of these activities, so I also had to write the printer control software from scratch.

Figure 7.2: LED six digit display. The top image shows the viewable face that may be arranged either as two groups of 3 digits each (not shown) or three groups of 2 digits each (as shown). The bottom image is the back, i.e., the component side, of the circuit board. Note that the unit is mounted on a piece of polycarbonate, plastic. The cross section view would be similar to that shown on the left side in Figure 10.3 on page 125. (SOURCE: A personal photos.)

Then I was told that there had to be some sort of large display to let the machine operator know the length of material as it unrolled. This was actually fun to make. I used large 4 inch high LEDs with a clever method of controlling the digits to be displayed as shown in Figure 7.2. Rather than use any type of information transmitter or receiver, I designed a unit containing a couple of inexpensive logic chips and programmed the Z-8000 to put out an encoded signal that the chips would shift, bit-by-bit

7.1 The carpet unroller

into registers controlling each of the 7-segment displayed digits.[1] All I needed to connect the display to the Z-8000 were just 4 wires, two for power and two for the encoded signal. This technique worked better than I expected.

We tried out the unit on an actual machine, and it worked relatively well. He then wanted me to make additional functionality. The next "new feature" the unit needed to do was to output information to a computer so that inventory updating could be done on the main office computer. If I could have ever felt sorry for a computer, it was this poor Z-8000 that would be the perfect candidate. While all this stuff was going on, I periodically would have to go to a client's facility to help install his main flooring computer and programs. I remember one time I had to drive from Little Rock to Dallas with my car loaded with equipment and work all day in a warehouse where the temperature was well over 100 degrees. Then halfway home in Texarkana—where Texas meets Arkansas—my car's air conditioner went out, and I felt cooked to medium rare by the time I got home. Finally, after a couple of years working on this project, my boss decided it was taking too long so he ended the project. Out of work again. Yikes!

---

[1] Actually each display consisted of 7 segments plus a decimal point. Therefore a total of 6 bytes were outputted bit-by-bit in a unique self-clocking serial manner requiring only a single wire for data.

8
Dillards Days

8.1 Bulletin boards and Usenet

The early 1990s was just about the time when people were starting to use computers to communicate with one another. The graphics internet, i.e., the World Wide Web (WWW), had not yet come into existence, but people had alphanumeric terminals and early computers that one could connect a slow modem. This gave rise to what was known as "bulletin boards" systems (BBS) where people could post information on someone's computer that hosted the bulletin board. There was a popular BBS in the Little Rock area, and I got to know the guy who set it up. Everything was *Usenet* those days with many "news groups" were being set up primarily between college groups at first. There were no or very limited graphics except those one could make using the characters on their a keyboard. The communications was all via written messages.

One popular use for bulletin boards was to put program files on it that others could download and run. This was also about the time that Phil Zimmerman introduced his famous Pretty Good Privacy (PGP) encryption program that our government was not particularly keen about. I was beginning to dabble in encryption algorithms myself and found the subject fascinating. The fellow who owned the local bulletin board system and I decided to contact Phil Zimmerman to see if we could download PGP and put it on his BBS.[1] Phil told us where to get it,

---

[1]There were several Usenet groups on cryptography that a number of early programmers like Zimmerman hung out in. I found it fascinating to be able to communicate directly with these guys who would later become quite famous in cryptography

and so we downloaded it. The program itself was quite small—under a million bytes—but with the slow speed of the modems it took us over an hour just to download that one file. Today downloading a file of that size takes a fraction of a second.

The University of Arkansas in Little Rock (UALR) had a amazing 64,000 bit per second connection to the actual internet, and this fellow who operated the BBS arranged to tap into the university's system because he had a close friend down there in the computer services department. I remember one day I was at his house, and we first tried out the system and were able to get into systems in Japan, Brazil, and other foreign countries. It was amazing.

8.2 Getting a job through the BBS contact

There was one "news group" in Little Rock that I participated in regularly. One of the participants was a young lady enrolled in computer science at the university. She was telling me about the subjects that she was taking and was fascinated by my computer background. When she learned I was unemployed she asked me if I had ever looked at Dillards Department Stores since I had a background both in retailing and programming. I told her I had, but they had no openings at present. She told me a relative, an uncle or someone, who was a vice president there and she would put in a good word about me. A month or two passed, and she arranged for me to have another job interview for which I was indebted. I ended up getting a programming job there.

Dillards Department Stores is headquartered in Little Rock, and they were heavy into computers. They had several hundred stores and were expanding on a regular basis. One of the neatest things I saw there was a room with a giant screen where they could watch every credit card transaction occurring company-wide in the organization. The corporation was an IBM shop meaning everything was IBM. This included the PC "windows-type" operating system called OS/2.

My job was to do programming using, of all things, COBOL. I hid my dislike of the language and went at the new job with enthusiasm. They had a very systematic way of programming where every program had to fit a pre-established pattern. It was like a one-size fits all approach

---

circles.

8.2 Getting a job through the BBS contact

with no programmer creativity involved. But it was a job after all, and beggars can't be choosers. While there I made a number of new friends, and we would talk about, of all things, computers. Gradually they got to know about my abilities from our conversations.

But Dillard's was not the only computer company in town. Acxiom Corporation, the largest such company, was headquartered in Conway, about a thirty-minute drive northwest of Little Rock. Acxiom was known for reducing its staff by hundreds of people if business was slow and then hiring back hundreds of new people when business picked up again. Such actions would always hit the local newspapers. When they start hiring they'd attempt to lure programmers away from other computer-oriented firms in the region.

One of my new friends at Dillards was hired away by Acxiom. I didn't think much about it at the time and just wished him good luck. It came as a complete surprise to me when one day he called me and told me he had told one group at Acxiom about me, and they wanted to interview me. I immediately said yes. They were very interested my background and offered me a position that I accepted without hesitation. Good bye to the drudge work programming COBOL and off, once again, to greener pastures. My total time at Dillards was just a little over a year and a quarter. I worked at Acxiom for about seven years.

9

Acxiom Days

Acxiom had a staff of hundreds and hundreds of programmers. Their business was information warehousing. If you lived in America, the chances are great that they had a file on you that is hundreds, if not thousands, of bytes long. They work with the three top credit bureaus—Transunion, Experian, and Equifax—and hence know all about you. Of course, all this information is highly confidential and kept as such.

Most people have gotten mail solicitations for credit cards from one of the major U.S. banks. There is an excellent chance that such a bank is a customer of Acxiom. For example, a bank would decide it would like to send a credit card application to all professional women between the ages of 35 and 45 who have children, are unmarried, and have a good credit record. The bank would submit these criteria to Acxiom, and Acxiom in turn would "mine" their database for all people who meet these specifications. If you met these specifications, you would get a "pre-approved" application in the mail. It was a very focused approach to marketing and a good way to maximize results at a relatively low cost.

The Digital Equipment Corporation (DEC) had introduced a new computer system called Alpha based on Microsoft Windows software. The main feature was that multiple processors could be used to yield an extremely powerful system. Acxiom decided to use an Alpha-based system and needed a systems programmer who knew assembly language to help with system development. They put some of their top programmers on the project. The drawback was that a few of the programmers thought they knew more than the other programmers which is not an ideal situation. The powers to be broke the project up into teams with a team leader.

9.1 When a team is not a team

I had worked quite successfully within a team approach at Telemed. I've always found the way to get the maximum work effort out of an employee is to motivate them to *wanting* to do something rather than *having* to do something.[1] This not only worked at Telemed but also at IITRI and in my fund-raising activities in Dixon as well as elsewhere. You have to get the people to buy into what they are doing and giving orders is not the way to do that. Motivating people is an art; some people have it, and some don't. Successful leaders have to be members of a team, not regarded as a leader of it. It's like herding cats. I'm reminded of a ball cap I used to have that had two brims pointing in different directions. The caption on the cap read, *I'm their leader, which way did they go?*

Unfortunately, many of the team leaders I encountered at Acxiom were people who, like with the other team leaders at Telemed, considered themselves to be managers who needed to micromanage the people under them. The team leader would know the best solution and dictate that the rest of the team must employ that approach even if it was not the best way to accomplish the goal at hand. In my opinion, it was a dictatorial approach and not the way an ideal team should work. However, to attempt to do things in the appropriate "corporate way," I tried my best to work within the system and not make waves (most of the time). Unfortunately, one person did part company with Acxiom due to my complaint that the team was not functioning as a true team should.

I got quite irritated once when one of my fellow workers ran into problems with the operating system. He was dead sure he knew how to fix the problem by randomly guessing on how to fix the problem rather than attempting to systematically determine where the problem lay. That was not my approach to solving a problem when an operating system misbehaved.

---

[1] I'll never forget the president at Telemed who had headed other large companies and had a MBA from Harvard telling me one time that he'd never seen a team like mine successfully tackle difficult tasks. He added that my form of leadership goes against what he was taught in graduate school but was so effective he wondered how I did it.

9.2 Read the damn manual

With our multiprocessor system, one severe problem that we encountered was trying to synchronize tasks between the multiprocessors. The Alpha system we were using was configured with four processors running separate intertwined tasks. The programmers were perplexed as to why the system was giving weird results that seemed to change on consecutive trial runs. They tried everything they could think of to find out what was going on but were stumped as to a solution.

When running into this sort of migrating problem, I normally hit the detailed manuals on how the internals work on the machine language level. Through carefully reading I discovered that prior to any attempt to do cross task synchronization, a special instruction must be given to get all four machines to complete their currently executing instructions. I did just this. After the different tasks on all the processors had stored their results, then communications between tasks on different machines would work seamlessly as expected. The result of the inclusion of this single instruction fixed the problem, and all was working smoothly after that. I got very little recognition for my efforts but that was okay, I was not really looking for praise but rather was just trying to get the project beyond that bottleneck. I did wonder, however, why all those other experienced programmers couldn't have figured this out without my help.

9.3 Toastmasters at Acxiom

While at Acxiom, I joined Toastmasters and benefitted tremendously from this move. I had not previously heard of this international organization, but it was supposed to make people better leaders and communicators. There were a lot of good speakers in the Acxiom club, and I learned a lot. The organization is subdivided into a well organized hierarchy going upward from member to club to area to division to district to national. I never reached the national level but held, at one time or another, all club to district positions usually many times over. I eventually became District Governor, covering a territory of all of Arkansas, one-third of Tennessee, and half of Mississippi and over 1,500 members. I do have a wall full of award plaques for outstanding performance in each of the positions I held. I continued in the organization well after I left Acxiom and finally stopped my membership after 25 years of being a Toastmaster.

Acxiom had an internal web-based system for corporate use. We decided to have a website on this network and so I set out to make one. This was my introduction to the Hypertext Markup Language commonly referred to as HTML, the basis for all webpages today. Like I usually did, I bought a couple of books on the subject and started studying. The language is called a markup language because it essentially "marks up" text as to how it is to be displayed. Today most people who use word processors like Microsoft's Word or Apple's Pages produce their webpages using a "word processor type" program so they don't have to remember all the basic HTML commands. I prefer to do mine using good old fashion HTML. Maybe it's because I'm used to programming fast in assembler language where I have more low level control as opposed to FORTRAN or COBOL. This being said, it all depends on the application to be programmed. By the way, one high level language that produces very efficient code—and is used when programming many operating systems—is 'C' which I love because of its power and efficiency.

So I put up a website on the Acxiom in-house network. I didn't realize at the time that this experience would provide me with an additional talent I have used extensively since learning it. When I got into higher levels in Toastmasters I implemented a website for our entire District that relied on using databases to hold the required information. I never got into real database design at Acxiom but would do so in the coming years.

9.4 Seeking greener pastures once again

I loved the 30 minute drive from Little Rock to Conway and back each day. I enjoyed this drive even more so in the fall of the year when the autumn colors would come out in their full glory. But all good things must come to an eventual end, and this one did quite unexpectedly. Acxiom was to undergo one of their periodic mass firings. I thought my position was safe, but I had just completed the project I was working on, when all the supervisors were told to cut their non-essential staff members.

One morning I was escorted into my supervisor's office and said that effective immediately I no longer worked there. I was one of several

9.4 Seeking greener pastures once again

hundred people they laid off over a period of a week or so. They did not even allow me to return to my office but rather escorted to the door of the building and was told they would pack up all my personal stuff and I could pick that up later. The human resources person told me it was not due to inadequate job performance but rather was due to corporate financial pressures. My termination records would state I was eligible for re-employment at the company once they started hiring again. That was nice to hear. Acxiom did provide significant help to those let go and hired an outside firm to give a week-long seminar on how to get a new job elsewhere. I met others at the seminar who had been with the company far longer than I had which was gratifying in a way.

I subsequently drove up to Conway in a day or two and picked up all my personal items neatly packed in several boxes. At the time I didn't realize it but about half of my 4-drawer file cabinet was filled with Toastmasters material that they never bothered to pack. In a strange twist of events, the loss of this material led me to another job. However, that will have to wait until after I make a slight detour to discuss something else I did while working at Acxiom, but not for Acxiom, that I found a very interesting challenge.

10

Calculator project

I have a good friend, Ed Lawton, in Dixon whose father hired me for my first job while in high school. Ed is a half year older than I am, and we became good friends for over half a century. I worked for that company, a local dairy, for my last two years in high school. During my senior year, I was given the job to manage about a dozen people in two of their retail stores.

When I had returned to Dixon after my father died, Ed and I made an attempt to set up a small computer service bureau which we never got off the ground. Whereas I went back into computer work after closing our store, his training was in business and he continued in his family business only to be forced to close in the next few years due to union problems. He started learning about doing income tax work and became very proficient at it. He ended up in St. Petersburg, Florida, spending half his time there and the other half back in Dixon where he owned a house. Over the years his tax business grew. In addition he became a tax advisor to some small to medium sized businesses. His business experience paid off in that respect.

During tax season Ed hired about a half dozen people or more to help him process tax returns. That was the time when a person could get a loan on his or her expected refund, and this activity was generally referred to as the "fast tax" business. The problem he was facing is that he was limited on the number of computers in his office. One day we were talking, and he told me his situation. I don't remember who it was to suggest it, but the idea of a specialized IRS Form 1040 tax calculator came up. This was in 1992 before modern phones like the iPhone and others were available so we had to develop our own device. Ed knew the tax business backward and forward, and I knew likewise about computers. So we decided to give it a try.

10.1 Calculator design phase

I had never before worked with a microcomputer. The difference between a microprocessor and a microcomputer is that a microprocessor only has a central processor on the chip and requires external memory, whereas a microcomputer has a limited amount of memory and data on the same chip. It literally is a full system on a single chip. This sounded intriguing to me to try to use that approach. I would also need a small liquid crystal display (LCD), a battery holder, and a circuit board that I could easily design. Oh yes, and a keypad. I could likewise design one using small switches for the keys. I was eager to try my hand at it. Still working for Acxiom, it would be a perfect evening/weekend project.

I'd like to deviate slightly at this point and explain a little something general about transistors. If your cell phone or other battery operated device were to use the older type transistors you would drain the battery in minutes. This is because the first transistors were "current" operated devices. Such devices consume a lot of power. Realizing this was a problem, a newer type of transistor was developed called a "field effect transistor" or just FET. Rather than rely on current, this new type relied on voltages and consumed practically no electric current but rather just voltage potential, i.e., voltage levels, to turn the transistors on and off. Without FETs, none of the portable electronic devices common today would be possible. A FET transistor only uses billionths of an amp for power—very low indeed! They are widely used in large computers today. Through development they have become as fast or faster than the older power hungry devices of years past.

So I looked around at various microcomputers and selected a Motorola FET-based device as shown in Figure 10.1. It was an 8-bit byte oriented machine entirely contained on one 40-pin computer chip and had very limited little number processing ability except for add, subtract capabilities and, of course, no operating system. The prime use of a chip like this would be to control traffic lights and the like—very simple applications. Unlike the old UNIVAC, the chip was capable of producing interrupts indicating that something external to it had occurred.

10.1 Calculator design phase

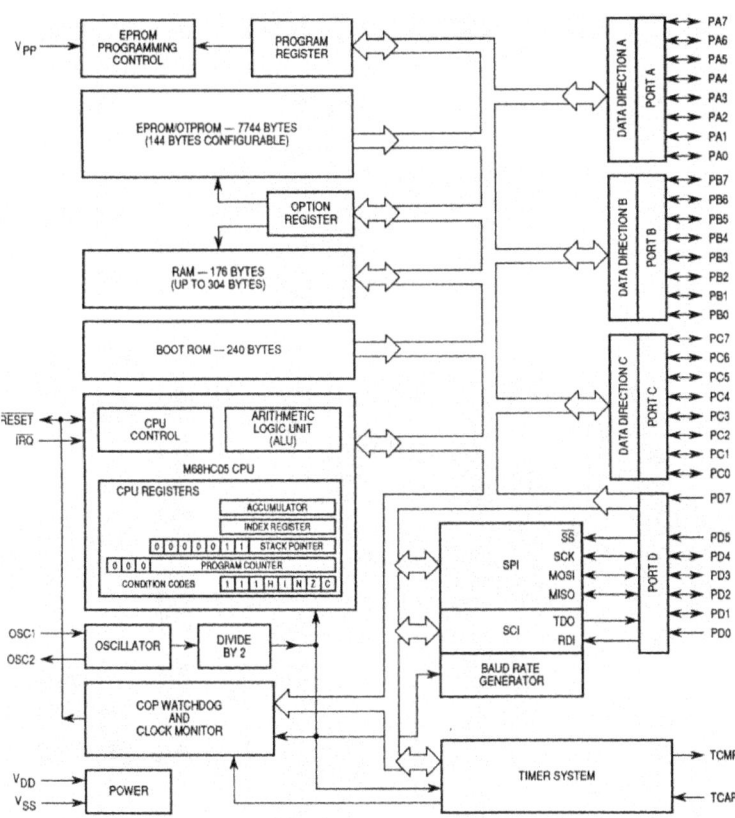

Figure 10.1: A block schematic of the Motorola microcomputer I selected for our calculator project. On the top left are shown the eProm (Erasable Programable Read Only Memory) memory to hold the read-only program and RAM (Random Access Memory) memory for holding working data. On the right are the 3 8-bit byte registers for communication with the LCD display and keypad along with the control lines that were required.(SOURCE: Motorola MC68HC705C8 technical databook.)

The one nice feature it had was three 8-bit registers for input and output of which I used every single available bit. I could utilize one of these to control external devices—like the LCD display and home-built keypad. I could use some of these bits to send data control signals to the display. And other of the bits could be used for detecting when one of the keypad keys was pressed. Not much else was required by our calculator. And it really didn't need an operating system of any type, a definite advantage for a calculator.

Tax calculation required long numbers and the capability to multiply and divide. I could do this in software—remember, practically any hardware logic can be done with software logic if one knows how, and I did. Interestingly, I could power the LCD display, which used field effect transistors (FETs) that had extremely low power requirement, and I could power the entire display with one control output bit. In this manner I just turned one of the output control lines off and the device's power would be shut off immediately thus saving battery power.

 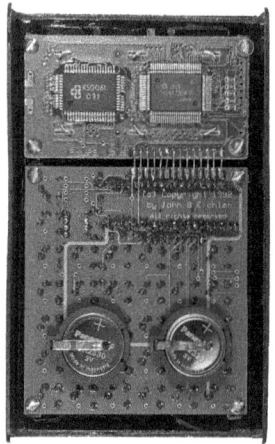

Figure 10.2: Calculator circuit board details. On the left is a picture of the keypad switches on the top-side of the board. On the right is a completed solder-side view of the calculator showing how the batteries were mounted. At the top is the LCD display unit (bought as a completed unit) and the small soldered wires connecting it to the main circuit board. (SOURCE: Personal photographs.)

I was limited severely by a 7,744 byte program memory, very tiny for a application like this. The question was: could I squeeze all of the information for an IRS Form 1040 into such a small memory? All the IRS tax tables—if you've ever looked at the instruction portion of the IRS tax tables you'll know what I mean—had to fit. Luckily, there are formulas that the IRS provides to calculate out the tax tables. Also it had only 176 bytes of read/write RAM memory to hold data in. I decided I'd give it a try and, as it turned out, I used every single byte, and I mean *every* last one.[1]

---

[1] To tell the truth, there was one obscure tax calculation where I needed to display

10.1 Calculator design phase

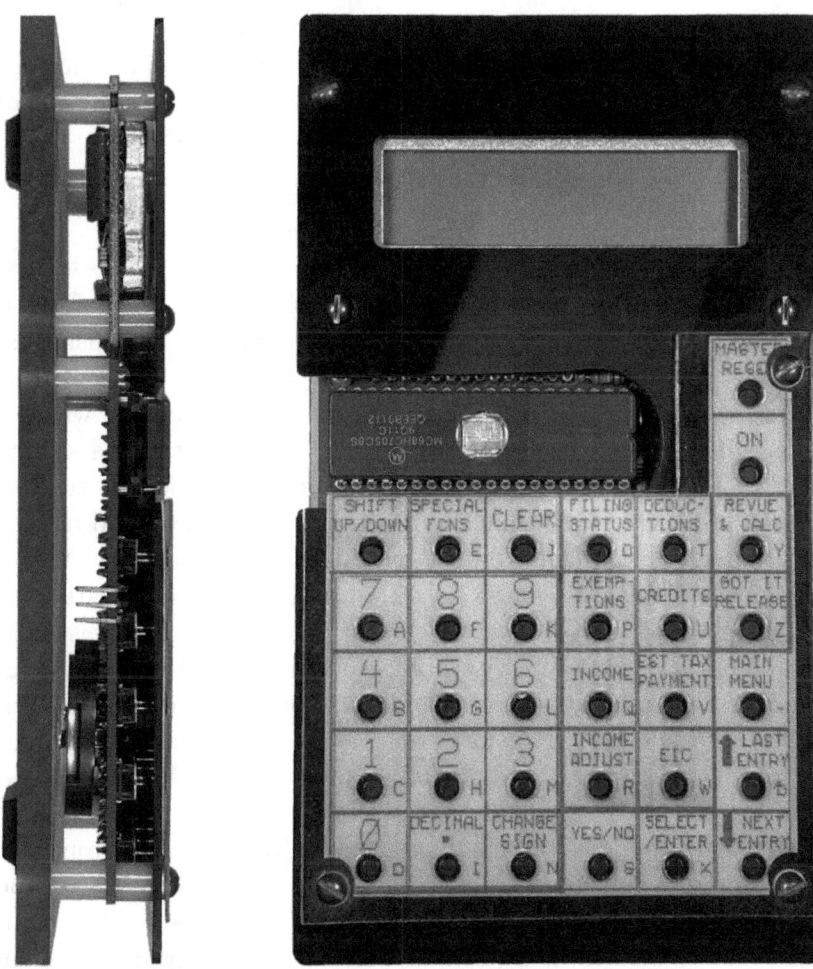

Figure 10.3: The calculator test rig. On the left is shown a side view of the device mounted on a piece of polycarbonate. On the right is a top view. I cut out a section of the top to provide easy access to the microcomputer IC. (SOURCE: Personal photographs.)

I designed the input keypad with small individual switches. As you might guess, inserting all those buttons and hand soldering them in was a real pain (but it was cheap!). If we had purchased any kind of custom-made keypad the expense would be quite large for all the keys we needed

---

a decimal point but couldn't find an extra byte anywhere to put coding for the darned thing.

and connecting it to our circuit board would present new problems. Besides we were going to produce a relatively small number of calculators. The circuit board I designed is shown in Figure 10.2. About the only other component on it was the microcomputer chip itself.

10.2 Programming the device

The next task was to code and debug our program. To perform this testing I could get one version of the microcomputer we were using as an electrically programmable device that could be erased and reused. For the final version we used the same microcomputer but in a write-only version which was much less expensive. I built a test rig as shown in Figure 10.3. You can see the small circular quartz window on the top of the integrated circuit (IC). The entire program memory could be erased by placing the chip under an ultraviolet light.

We had to make a case to hold the unit. Once again, rather than purchasing a ready-made case, which would be expensive, it was decided to make our own out of black polycarbonate. For this we bought a number of custom cut pieces of the plastic, some for the front and equal number for the back. Polycarbonate is one of my favorite materials because it is easily made and virtually indestructible. I also could bend it in a vise nicely. We did have to send the tops out to a machine shop to get precision drilling of the holes we needed. To attach the front to the back I simply used a special plastic liquid adhesive. The nice part about this is that with the aid of a highly specialized tool called a kitchen knife, I could readily detach the front from the back for battery replacement if needed. We never needed to do that, thank goodness.

10.3 The finished calculator

Figure 10.4 shows the completed calculator. To identify the keys, I created a pattern and had it printed on adhesive backed sheets of film that the backing could be peeled off and affixed to the top. Then we started our "mass produced" assembly line of my wife and myself putting the dozen or so devices together on our kitchen table.

I designed the device in the fall of 1992, and Ed used them quite successfully for the 1993 tax season at his business in Florida that year.

10.3 The finished calculator

As I was writing this chapter I wondered if the device I had on hand would still function. Of course, the batteries in the unit had died years ago. So I plopped two new batteries into the unit, and it came to life instantly. It went through its test function asking for all the keys to be consecutively pushed—I wrote that into the program so I had a way of testing units after assembly—and then showed my copyright information and then was ready for tax information input. After almost 30 years of sitting dormant it still worked!

Figure 10.4: Our completed tax calculator. (SOURCE: Personal photograph.)

I got great satisfaction in building a specialized calculator from scratch. I truly love product development.

11

Election Resources Days

I mention at the end of Chapter 9 that the HR person from Acxiom who packed my things forgot about the personal stuff in my file cabinet. After this happened I contacted Acxiom HR and inquired if I could get my Toastmasters material back. They search in vain for it but couldn't locate it.

The HR rep asked how my job search was proceeding and I told him I was having problems locating a new position. He mentioned that he had a good friend in Little Rock in an employment agency that I might contact, and furthermore, he'd give her a call to help set up an appointment for me. I told him I would greatly appreciate him doing so, and I gave her a call and drove out to chat with her.

After meeting with her she said that she was searching for someone for a small company located very close by where I live. She called them while I was at her office and then told me that she had set up an appointment for me that afternoon.

Election Resources Corporation (ERC) was essentially a mom-and-pop family business that had been around for years. Aside from the owner, his wife, and their daughter worked for the company as did one other programmer, a whiz at database design, and his daughter. I high-tailed it over to talk with them in the afternoon.

I told them my background. ERC had a nationwide reputation as being experts in the field of elections. They had developed a quite sophisticated computer program with information about candidates and ballot issues that would be inputted and the proofs for the ballot would be spit out the other end. ERC would only produce the proofs for the ballots, and it was up to the county to have them printed.

Producing ballots was an art which most people don't appreciate. The national offices and senate candidate would be state-wide on all ballots. But that is where simplicity ends. Each voter is located in a physical district, and those overlap since this is dependent on how district borders were drawn. This means that for each voting precinct there may be a number of different ballots required. In fact, your neighbor might well be voting a different ballot because of how districts are divided. ERC's program would take all of this into consideration when producing ballots. Another problem which might pop up is different languages. Specialized ballots might be required if different languages are spoken in a single precinct. For example, one time we were producing ballots for one California county that we had four languages and had to generate a total of 6,800 different ballots.

11.1 My first project at ERC

Election Resources had just landed a contract to design all the ballots for one of the larger western mountain states. The original intent was to make a cut-down "lite" version[1] of their program for each of the 65 counties in the state. Doing so, they would be getting output data from all of the counties. ERC needed someone to take that data and put it into a form from which we could produce the final ballots. In the job interview I was asked if that would be something I would be interested in. I responded yes. I was then asked if I could start that afternoon to which I again responded in the affirmative.

To give all these "lite" versions of their program—which did not produce the final ballots but would be used for data input only—would be a nightmare to manage. But they had to get a workable solution for getting such information for the upcoming 2000 general election, and this was the only solution they could think of for such a large project. One thing in my favor was that I was familiar with database design having

---

[1] A lite version of a computer program is generally a version not containing all of the features of the original version. For example, commercial software companies often offer a lite version of their program at reduced cost with consumers required to pay more for the full version. With ERC's software, not all the features of the full version would be needed for the task at hand so much of the program would not be included in the lite version.

done a good deal of it in the work I did for the Toastmasters district-wide website I had put together. I completely understood what they had in mind.

Databases are organized in interrelated tables. Whereas I had just used a couple of tables with the Toastmaster project, ERC's databases had something like 25 tables which were massive in comparison. So I started to learn about their system. Luckily the other programmer they had working for them was an absolute genius when it comes to database design so I couldn't screw up things too badly. Several weeks went by, and I was enjoying the work.

11.2 A sudden change in direction

The owner of ERC was a great guy to work for and every week he'd take us programmers out for lunch. During lunch we generally discussed the project and the challenges it presented. I said things would be much easier just to do it via the Internet. They asked me what I meant. I said I'd set up a website, and then a county could just enter its data in fields on a webpage. They asked if they could do that, and I said yes, it would be a snap—not literally but certainly it wouldn't be that hard to do. Their response was, "Could you do that?" I told them sure. No one in the company knew much about webpage design—it was relatively new at the time—and so I got a new assignment. Thank goodness for my Toastmaster experience in doing web work.

I usually start webpage design by opening a text editor, not a word processing program, on my computer. If I was to type a hundred character sentence in a word processor such as Microsoft Word or Apple Pages, I would be lucky if it produced a file under twenty thousand bytes in size. Word processors put in tons of extra data besides from just the hundred characters I typed. A text editor—examples are 'textpad' in Windows and 'textedit' on a Mac—outputs only the characters entered. Of course, there are special characters like carriage returns and line feeds that are also stored, but those are stored as 1-byte values. That takes care of my editing program: very plain, very simple, and very free.[2] I

---

[2]While discussing text editors, my all-time favorite is UltraEdit that is available on either a Windows or Mac computer. This program can do almost anything, and I love it because of its power. I would go so far to say it can do anything except wash the dishes or bake a cake. I started using UltraEdit at ERC and have stuck with it

write my HTML lines—very few to begin with—and then save the file as a .html or .htm file, both work equally as well.

Next, I open a standard browser like Chrome, Firefox, Safari, etc., and use the browser option—that all browsers have—to open a local file on the computer being used. I would open the .html or .htm file, and I'd be ready to start writing my HTML webpage code. After writing some additional HTML code with my text editor, I just save it and do a refresh, i.e., refresh my browser, and immediately see the results of my added HTML. All then required for webpage design are two simple programs all computers have that either come with the system or may be downloaded free. One doesn't even need a webpage account with a hosting company to get started in forming the webpage. In either a Windows or Apple Mac machine, multiple windows may be worked on without closing them, so I just pick the window, edit or browser, and I'm in business.

11.3 The data input program webpage

I cleaned and formatted the user input into a form that it could easily be added to the master database. I had to be very careful that any typos an input typist might make didn't corrupt the database. This was essential. I never assume any input—especially from a human at a keyboard—to be error-free. I have found anyone who assumes input data does not contain errors is ready for a sad learning experience. People make errors and expecting otherwise is treading in dangerous territory. From working with computers for so many years it may seem strange that I harbor a suspicion of them. I've gotten into the habit of always double and triple checking what computers spit out.

An all-time great example of this was at Boise Cascade. Before their new IBM 360 system, Boise used what is termed 'unit record' equipment based on putting all their records on punched cards. With punched cards a shortcut to correct a wrong punch, in many cases, is to re-punch the bad column in the card having a problem. This worked because they knew the card reader had the idiosyncrasy of reading the punched holes in a particular order and they could fool the equipment. The operators

---

ever since. It is not the least expensive text editor but years ago I bought a lifetime license and so all my updates are free to me so was well worth the expense in my mind.

knew these little tricks and used them over the years. Anything to save a little time. But computers can't be fooled so easily.

When their computer arrived, one of the COBOL programmers wrote a program to read in these thousands upon thousands of cards to load them into a digital file on the new computer. This would, in many cases, take four or five hours to read in a batch of these cards. COBOL is lousy when it comes to being able to check all the input fields for invalid column punches, This would stop the system cold when an invalid column was detected sometimes after reading in thousands of cards over several hours. The card in error was fixed, and then they would have to start all over. Then another bad card would stop the system again, and the procedure was started from scratch all over again. Seeing this was a major problem, I wrote a simple assembly language program that read in all the cards and then flagged those records in error so they could be fixed saving much time and frustration.

But now back to ERC. I finished my input program which the users in all our client state's counties used to input their candidate and ballot issues without having to distribute a "lite" version of ERC's program to all the counties. As it turned out a goodly number of the counties couldn't even manage to get their data entered, and we had to enter it for them at our office using the web-based system which we had not anticipated. Anyway, my portion of the coding worked, and I was happy with the result. I still think if we had distributed a "lite" version of ERC's more complicated program there would have been a greater number of problems.

11.4 Working with a perfectionist boss

The owner of ERC was a perfectionist when it came to user data entry. He did not micromanage—a common trait of many lesser managers who feel their management skills were required for everything—but would quickly notice if something took extra keystrokes to do. I gradually learned a lot from his keen eye in this regard. I have always been aware of the importance of making user interfaces for computers. But my boss was instinctually an expert on this topic. Those extra messages one often encounters like "Are you sure that you want to save the file" or "Do you really want to delete this file" drove him nuts. Of course there are times when such warnings are desirable but too many are frustrating to good accurate typists.

I've grown to learn that it is not enough just to have a program work. It is important that it works smoothly as far as the user is concerned. Not having a smooth user interface is usually the result of a programmer being just too plain lazy to take the time to do it properly. Another example is when a user takes the time on a webpage to enter form information and then it is rejected for a single field in error. Good interface design is to only allow the user to correct the single field in error. Bad interface design is when the program clears of all form data previously entered resulting in everything having to be entered again. My only advice to programmers is that, in the long run, it pays to take the time to do it right. Refine, refine, refine.

While on this subject of programming practices, I'd like to mention one other related practice that troubles many programmers. Documentation of programs is important. When such documentation is written as a separate document, i.e., separate from the program itself, it frequently occurs that over a period of time that documentation is lost. This is especially true if a program has been running properly over a period of years, and then suddenly a problem pops up. It's usually a mad scramble to figure out where the problem is in a program that was written years before. So I write detailed documentation for myself as much as for anyone else. Great habit to acquire if you're a programmer!

As a result I have always made it a long standing practice to document the program in the program itself in the form of comments. I write a comment on almost every line of coding except when I'm doing a quick program that is only to be used once and time is critical. This has saved the day many a time when I'm called upon to go over coding that is years old. It also helps when a new programmer is charged with making program modifications after the original coder has moved on to a new job. Some programmers feel that they have added job security if fewer comments are made internal to the code itself. I've always thought this is a false sense of security and greatly limits a programmer if some new position opens within a company but management is hesitant about giving it to a person because they are so vital to keeping a system running. Don't fall into this trap. Always make your coding so complete that it can be turned over to someone else if a new opportunity presents itself. Enough preaching.

11.5 Election night results

Our client Secretary of State wanted to use ERC's web system to input results of the 2000 general election and then have a mechanism to periodically get the results during the night of the election to have them posted on the state's SOS's state-run website. This was fine, and I knew the concept was sound. I wrote a program to allow people at the SOS office to input election results continuously during the night of the election as fast as the results come in. I wrote a second program that could be run every half hour or so producing the required webpages automatically to be sent back to the SOS office. I made my program to automatically create some 480 files and put them all together into one big file they could download. I made another small program that they could run which would subsequently break all the files into individual ones they could easily upload to their web-based system. This worked out quite well, and they were very happy with the procedure. Although not directly related to computers per se, Appendix B on page 155 goes into more detail, in an understandable manner, on how the election reports are interconnected through an extensive use of hyperlinks. I included this appendix to give an idea of the complexities of processing election data which I found extremely interesting.

11.6 One nasty bug remained

Since data input was a prime factor, we tested the reporting system extensively at our office employing everyone typing in simulated computer election results to see if we could break the system. Better us break it than the customer. We spent weeks on testing.

Everyone at the ERC office was about burned out by the tedious testing, but we thought we were ready for election day. All systems seemed to work as planned. But to make sure we wanted one last test on election day. During the day I had people typing in test data like mad, and all of a sudden the results coming out weren't working in producing accurate tallies of the input data. I was panicked. What possibly could the problem be? The polls would be closing in a matter of hours so I started to try to locate the problem. It was very important that ERC looked good to the SOS's office.

I finally found the problem. When passing data between a user and a web program there are two ways to do it, one using the HTML 'get' command and the other using the 'put' command. If you've ever noticed, sometimes following the Universal Resource Locator (URL) you will see a '?' character followed by some data—usually encoded so you don't know what it means—and sometimes not. In one case the 'get' command used was for short data like a few hundred bytes and in the other case the data is sent via a separate mechanism for larger amounts of data for the 'put' command. I was using the 'get' rather than the 'put' command which resulted in not getting all the input data to the receiving program. This was happening in our case. During the final testing we used much more data in sending it to the computer for analysis.

Luckily, I realized this error, and it was an easy one to correct. A relatively simple fix was to just change the way the data was sent by changing all 'get's to 'put's. It took only a few minutes to perform the HTML code modification. We retested, and it worked great. In the end everyone was happy, and I got a well deserved but completely unexpected substantial bonus for my efforts. The company got high marks for its efforts in the 2000 general election.

11.7 A "Big brother is watching you" program

It is important that election software work in a flawless manner. One of our clients insisted that the software we used must comply with a rigid set of standards and hired a consultant to ensure it happen. A man from a separate company was hired and would monitor our software development.

This was something new to me. Every subroutine written must conform to this set of standards they had set. At the beginning of each such subroutine had to have an elaborate description of the function that subroutine performed. All the input and output had to be spelled out in detail. Since I liked to do in-program documentation, it was not hard to fulfill these requirements. But, they were tedious to say the least. I thought it was an excellent idea and fully complied with doing it "by the book." I was just happy that such strict documentation was not required in any of the other positions I've held over the years. But, I could really see a real need for program standards.

Additionally, I've always had a thing for security and had studied cryptography out of a general interest in the subject. In fact, while working for Acxiom I wrote one of the first message digest programs—on my own time for my personal use—that was certified by the National Institutes of Standards and Technology (NIST) which had been previously known as the National Bureau of Standards (NBS). A message digest is essentially a "fingerprint" for a file. Such digests are widely used to ensure not one bit in a file had been changed. It's a security thing for and used for legal purposes.

All the big computer companies had written such certified software. But implementing it could be on either a byte basis or a bit basis. I did it on a bit basis. If you were to search the NIST database for Secure Hashing Algorithm (SHA) implementations you will find that my program was number two in the list (National Semiconductor was the first) and the only one of hundreds at that time that was done on a bit basis.

11.8 Ready to give up the ship

In 2005 I was 66 years old, and my wife had already retired. I enjoyed the work but figured it was time that I think about retirement. Election Resources was sold to Sequoia Voting Systems, one of the leaders in the election field.[3] They were going to close the Little Rock office but said that I could work from home if I so desired. I was ready for a change and decided then was as good a time as any to skip the day-to-day hubbub associated with work in the computer field. I had worked over 45 years in a field doing work I loved every minute of the day (and night). So I told my boss that I felt it was time to hang up my hat and pursue other activities and I opted for retirement.

---

[3]It was sold several other times after that. Thus ERC was eventually lost to the dust bin of history.

12

Retirement Days

Our oldest daughter, during her sophomore year in high school, told me that she was going to get a PhD in Psychology. She is quite a determined person who finally got her doctorate on the last day of the last century and now is a full professor at a local university. Several years prior to that she obtained her Masters degree and, of course, we attended the ceremony. Watching her I distinctly remember that I thought back over my some 35 years of working that I only had one course in computers at IIT and that was a desk-sized business machine and nothing in comparison to the huge UNIVAC that I worked on daily. The only thing I got out of that class was that computers can come in all sizes and I got a good grade in the course. Also, I believe I had more hands on computer experience than my instructor.

I'm an avid reader and taught myself virtually every thing I learned about programming and hardware design and I thought that I was pretty good at it. I am of the opinion that it's all in the books and manuals and anyone, if they dig deep enough, can learn just about anything. But sitting in that auditorium watching her graduate, I wondered what it would be like to take some computer classes at the University of Arkansas in Little Rock so I decided to check it out. This led to me taking a total of three courses in the computer science department: 'C' programming language, data structures, and operating system design. I thought at that time—being the oldest person in all these computer classes—that the other younger college students would run circles around me. Much to my surprise, after about two or three weeks, many of my fellow students would start asking me how to do things. I couldn't believe the limited knowledge some of these students had, especially those with majors in computer science. After my third class, one of the instructors in the computer department left, and I was hired to be an instructor in evening school, which I did for a couple of years. Back in the early 1960s I had previously taught a course in dynamics at IIT in the evening school for two years and enjoyed doing so.

12.1 Back to school

In the state of Arkansas anyone over 60 years of age can take free classes at any state university. Having reached that golden age in 1999, I thought I'd take advantage of this opportunity and looked at what classes I might find interesting.

I have a Toastmasters friend in Hot Springs, Arkansas. At one of the District conferences he gave a speech on voice projection. He was involved in local theater as a director and actor in plays produced in Hot Springs. Moreover, he really knew something about voice projection. I called the University of Arkansas in Little Rock (UALR) and asked about classes in this field. They had a voice class in the music department that sounded interesting and so I considered taking it. The person conducting the class said I would enjoy it if I didn't mind singing to the class. By the time I got around to registering the class was already filled.

So I looked at other potential classes to take. I definitely did not want to take any classes in the computer department since I was somewhat burned out on that topic. But I did find a class called Introduction to Creative Writing in the English department that sounded interesting. By this time of my life I had become a reasonably good typist and figured that writing fiction stories would be within my capabilities. So I registered for that class.

The instructor was a Professor David Jauss who himself was a published fiction writer and poet. I thought my first attempt at writing a short story was pretty darn good, but the advice I got from Jauss was to throw away the first 8 pages of my 13 page story. Wow, did I have a lot to learn! The fiction writing class could be taken repeatedly since each semester produced different stories. Besides, it was one of the few classes where I could get full credit for the course no matter how many times I took it. Jauss was so brilliant that I took his fiction writing course some 14 or so semesters and learned a lot.

12.1 Back to school

One day when I was talking to the head of the English department, he suggested that I look into getting a Masters degree in the Masters of Arts in Liberal Studies (MALS)—later to be renamed Masters of Arts in Interdisciplinary Studies (MAIS)—which I did and was accepted. At first I thought my grades at IIT would not be good enough to be accepted into the program as I had been a lousy student in undergraduate college. In my courses at UALR I got straight 'A's[1] so for the next few years I was once again a college student at UALR. I only took one or two classes each semester since work took up most of my time.

At IIT I had a double major—math and physics—and a double minor—psychology and business—so I was somewhat scientifically inclined. Over the years I had not lost my interest in science both in cosmology and geophysics. While attending classes at UALR I thought it might be worthwhile to put down some of my thoughts on those subjects in conjunction with my Masters. They had an "independent study" class that could be taken with a specified professor. When I suggested that I do some nonfiction writing, I was told I could not do it in the English department. Rather, it was suggested that I find someone in the Writing and Rhetoric department willing to work with me.

I approached faculty in that department, and they said, in essence, "Who are you?" I had never taken any courses in that department, and they didn't know me from Adam. So I registered for a course in memoir writing from Professor George Jensen the Department chair, which incidentally I put to good use when writing this book. The following semester I took a course in editing from Professor Chuck Anderson, the man I really wanted to do an independent study under. Toward the end of the semester I told Anderson that I would like to take such a study under his guidance, and he reluctantly agreed that I could try it for one semester which I did (in reality it stretched into two semesters). The result was a manuscript for a book on science. Chuck was an interesting person and concentrated on nothing but nonfiction writing. He was even an editor for a journal published by Johns Hopkins Medical School. I had a great time writing that year for him with many lively conversations. Although he is now retired, we have remained good friends.

For some reason I can't recall, I couldn't continue with the person I

---

[1] It is much easier the second time around when one has aged a bit and has some life and work experience under their belt. Don't ever think you are too old to learn. An old dog can be taught new tricks.

was working with as my advisor on my thesis so I asked Professor Anderson if he could do it, but he was too busy to take me on. He suggested that I ask a colleague of his in the department, Dr. David Fisher, if he would like to do it. Fisher said he would, so under his guidance, I took selected portions of my manuscript and elaborated on them turning them into my Masters thesis. Before I finally got my Masters, Fisher left UALR, and they got an advisor for me in the Philosophy department of all places. I ended up graduating with my Masters in 2015. My thesis is titled "Rhetoric and paradigm changes in science: Three case studies" and is freely available online. The actual manuscript I wrote in the independent study has a tentative title of "An Infinite Universe" and currently runs over 400 pages. I have yet to publish it though I'm still working on it and hope to do so one of these days.

12.2 My Interdata Collection

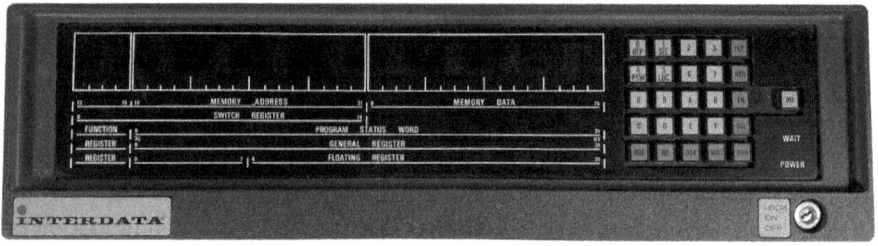

Figure 12.1: The Interdata console. Behind this console was a chassis that held 16 computer boards each being about 16 inches square. (Source: Personal photograph.)

In the late 1980s and early 1990s, new ECG carts could run an ECG analysis right in the cart itself. Some of the hospitals and clinics that had purchased Telemed's MEPC and EPIC systems, one even with the mass storage option, wanted to literally junk these now obsolete systems. A few places I assisted over the years contacted me and asked if I had any use for their old system, and if I did, to please come and haul it away.

I took advantage of this and obtained several systems, one even with two of the CDC 300 MB disk drives of the sort shown in Figure 4.5 on page 73. These massive disk units weighed around 550 pounds each, and

I had to find space in our basement to put them. When I got that one system I had to rent a 12 foot truck to transport it to Little Rock. Later I traded those two drives off to a Dallas firm for a couple of smaller 160 MB drives. I also acquired a couple of Interdata 5/16 machines that were used in the receiver on later versions of the EPIC system.

At this point I had accumulated perhaps the world's largest collection of Interdata equipment. I read that Paul Allen, co-founder of Microsoft was looking for old Interdata equipment for a computer museum he was creating in Seattle, Washington. I contacted the museum, and they were very interested. We came to an agreement, and they ended up getting about two tons of my Interdata equipment. Figure 12.2 shows my old computer that they have set up at the museum. I enlarged portions of Figure 12.2 in Figures 12.3 and 12.4 to show details hard to see in Figure 12.2. If you look at these figures closely you will notice the museum has powered up not only the computer but also one of my old displays.

This machine looks different from the EPIC systems because I made it with parts bastardized from a variety of different systems. I loaded it up with numerous memory boards and even modified one of the Interdata printer boards so it would work with an old dot matrix printer. I also made that machine communicate with an IBM 16-bit PC personal computer. At least I know now that the world will continue to enjoy the machine I spent years of my lifetime working on. I found a search for Interdata on Wikipedia also showed that photograph in Figure 12.2.

12.3 Other retirement activities

I still retain my interest in geophysics and have made several friends with the same interest around the world. In 2011 I published an article on that topic which obtained some interest. A friend named James Maxlow, a PhD geologist from Australia, has published several books on geology, two of which I edited for him. In both books he devotes a chapter on the theory I advanced in my 2011 article. In addition, I was asked by another friend in the U.K. to contribute a chapter in a book he was putting together on the subject, which I did, and it's now published. I have yet to reach the stage in retirement where I have spare time on my hands. I have already started work on a couple of other books on subjects that interest me. Retirement doesn't need be boring!

Figure 12.2: One of my old Interdata 7/32 machines now on display in the Living Computer Museum in Seattle. (SOURCE: Living Computer Museum photograph.)

Figure 12.3: Interdata console.(SOURCE: Living Computer Museum photograph.)

Figure 12.4: Display terminal.(SOURCE: Living Computer Museum photograph.)

12.4 Conclusion: Looking back

Looking back over my years working, I feel very lucky in getting in on the ground floor of the exponential growth of computers that are ubiquitous today. I also was fortunate in finding an occupation where I enjoyed going to work every day, even though at times I could (and did) swear at the way those damn computers were giving me fits and misbehaving. I had the good fortune of workng with and for some great people who gave me the latitude to pursue software and hardware development without trying to micromanage the way I performed the work toward reaching the desired goal.

My time at IITRI gave me a good "feel" for how to instrument systems, in the same way one would insturment an experiment, thus honing my skills in detecting hard-to-find problems. Working in our store in Dixon gave me the opportunity to develop my leadership skills particularly in running local civic organizations. Also Dixon provided training of how to handle difficult situations such as we encountered in rough retail waters. Telemed gave me a chance to develop and manage a technical group successfully that led to our group being recognized as the most productive in the company. ECG systems in Little Rock provided a platform to design and develop the fastest minicomputer ECG analysis system, at the time, in the world. I particularly enjoyed the fact that everything from hardware, to software, and even the operating system were products of my imagination. And finally, my time at Election Resources allowed me to implement a web-based system that a whole state used during the 2000 general election. If I had the chance to live my whole life over again, I resoundingly would reply yes without hesitation. Give me those *damn computers* any day of the week.

Appendices

Appendix A

Bits, nybbles, bytes, words: A primer

Fundamental to any discussion of computers is how they store information used for processing.[1] This appendix will explain how information storage works within a computer. The whole purpose is so when I discuss storage concepts you, the reader, will have a conceptual idea of what is being talked about. It's really not that complicated.

The basic element of storage in a computer is a single *bit*. A bit is nothing more that a switch that is either off or on. In computers the representation of a bit is either a 0 (zero) for off and a 1 (one) for on. This is referred to as a *binary* situation, i.e., only two states may occur. A single bit then can only represent one state or one *binary digit*, i.e., 0 or 1. As such a single bit is not very useful by itself.

To make some unit of storage useful, a series of bits are usually

---

[1]This appendix may at first look complicated but it is not. Read it slowly and understand each topic before going on to the next topic. There is only one fundamental rule which is that with 'n' bits one can represent only 2^n combinations of these bits. The number 2^2 (n = 2) means 2x2 (equals 4) and 2^3 (n = 3) means 2x2x2 (equals 8), and 2^4 (n = 4) means 2x2x2x2 (equals 16), etc. The is a very basic to understanding computers. The most common values that are encountered are: n = 8 equals 256, n = 16 equals 65,536, n = 32 equals 4,294,967,296 and n = 64 equals a very large number indeed. When speaking about a 16-bit computer that means that the computer transfers 16 bits at a time to/from memory and a 32-bit computer transfers 32 bits at a time to/from memory. In general, the more bits transferred at a time relates directly to the power of a computer. That is why early 8-bit computers are so difficult to program efficiently. It's that simple.

149

grouped together so some meaningful information may be stored by the group. The most common basic grouping on today's machines is the *byte* which contains 8 binary switches. But when the 1105 came out, as mentioned in the text, the byte had not yet been invented. Bytes only came into widespread use when IBM introduced their System 360 computer family in the mid 1960s. Hence, early computers grouped bits together in all kinds of weird groupings. There were 5-bit machines, 7-bit machines, 12-bit machines, 16-bit machine, etc.—in short there was a hodgepodge of different machines each usually directed toward specific end user applications.

A.1 Possible combinations of 'n' bits

Number of bits n	2^n	Calculation	Combinations
1	2^1	2x1	2
2	2^2	2x2	4
3	2^3	2x2x2	8
4	2^4	2x2x2x2	16
5	2^5	2x2x2x2x2	32
6	2^6	2x2x2x2x2x2	64
7	2^7	2x2x2x2x2x2x2	128
8	2^8	2x2x2x2x2x2x2x2	256

Table A.1: Number of combinations 2^n possible for 'n' bits

I want to start this discussion by taking an arbitrary grouping in 'n' bits where n may be any value. (It turns out that there are particular values of n that are of primary interest.) The question comes up as to how many combinations of binary digits can n digits represent. I'll tell you the answer ahead of time... it's 2^n. The number 2 is because we are talking about binary values. The number n is called an exponent, i.e., the number of 2s needed as we will see.

Column 1 of Table A.1 shows the the number of bits used, i.e., from 1 to 8. Column 2 shows 2^n where n is the value in column 1. Column 3 shows how to calculate the value in column 2. And finally column 4 shows the result of the calculation in column 3. Note that each value in column 4 is just double the previous value. What this means is to double a value all that needs to be done is to add one more bit to the left side of the binary number.

A.2 Common number bases used

To simplify the representation of binary numbers, different number bases are used. This means that string of binary zeros and ones may be expressed in more common number that are easier to write and read are utilized.

Table A.2 shows a grouping of 4 bits and all the possible combination of bit values for those 4 bits. Note that there are a maximum of 16 different bit—think switch—combinations of 4 bits. Column 2 shows the binary values for each combination. Just like in decimal digits, high order zeros may be dropped like 0050 is the same as 50. Column 2, if you add back the high order zeros, is identical to column 1.

The next three columns show the digits to various *bases*. If the base used is 10—the one our decimal number system is based on—there are 10 possible digits, i.e., 0 through 9. Once we use up all the combinations, we must add an additional digit to the left such as the 1 added to the number 0 to get 10, and so on. As is obvious in this table there are a total of 16 possible combinations of 4 bits and the decimal number system is clumsy since bit combinations 1010 through 1111 have no single digit representations.

Since computers use bits it makes sense to look for some numbering system to have a single digit representation without wasting some combinations. There are two such schemes commonly used: one to the base 8 and the other to the base 16 as shown in the last two columns. The octal number system has no 8s or 9s so when 7 is reached, an additional octal digits must be added as shown for the bit group of 1000. But that's okay since at the group of 1111 then next octal value would be 20 hence octal makes efficient usage of all bit combinations.

On the other hand, with hexadecimal one adds the "digits" A through F. I know this might seem strange at first but here A through F are regarded as digits rather than characters but doing this makes efficient use of all 16 possible binary combinations. Whenever a D is encountered, the computer interprets it as the 1101 bit combination. What seems, at first, somewhat strange that 4 plus 4 in octal is 10 and 8 plus 8 in hexadecimal is 10, etc.

Bit group	Binary (base 2)	Decimal (base 10)	Octal (base 8)	Hexadecimal (base 16)
0000	0	0	0	0
0001	1	1	1	1
0010	10	2	2	2
0011	11	3	3	3
0100	100	4	4	4
0101	101	5	5	5
0110	110	6	6	6
0111	111	7	7	7
1000	1000	8	10	8
1001	1001	9	11	9
1010	1010	10	12	A
1011	1011	11	13	B
1100	1100	12	14	C
1101	1101	13	15	D
1110	1110	14	16	E
1111	1111	15	17	F
1 0000	1 0000	16	20	10

Table A.2: Counting in different base number systems

A.3 Industry standardization

The early scientific computers—such as the UNIVAC 1105 and the IBM 7094—standardized on 36-bit word lengths. *Word* refers generally to the size of the group stored in the computer's memory and the size of *registers* used on the machine for performing operations. Even though 36 is evenly divisible by 4, one ends up with 9 hexadecimal digits which is an odd number. Because of this the octal number system was preferred where 12 octal (36 divided by 3) digits would represent completely one computer word.

When IBM introduced their System 360 computer family, they chose a 32-bit word which could be represented by 8 hexadecimal digits (32 divided by 4). The name applied to one grouping of 4 bits (one hexadecimal digit) became known as a *nybble* and 8 bits (2 nybbles) became known as a *byte*. After the mid 1960s when the System 360 was introduced, it rapidly became an industry standard to the present day.

The byte is a very convenient bit grouping. A single byte, D5 for example, represents the bit combination of 1101 0101. Nothing is lost! A single byte can contain a total of 16 times 16 combinations which is 256 (2^8), i.e., 0 through 255. Having 256 possible combinations is great since one byte can be used to encode the alphabet (A-Z) and (a-z) and (0-9) with plenty of unused combination for special characters such as '(' and '$' and '%', etc.). In this manner the one byte can contain all the commonly used alphanumeric and special characters and even printer control characters representing carriage returns, new lines, tabs, etc. This is the main advantage to use the hexadecimal numbering system.

As one can readily imagine, the longer the word length the more wire interconnections are required. To transfer a single byte only 8 wires are needed. This is why the very early integrated circuit computer-on-a-chip were primarily either 4-bit or 8-bit machines since the technology had not yet arrived to enable more complex electronic circuits. These chips were used primarily for simple control applications such as controlling a traffic light, etc. The next generation of computer chips could squeeze more circuitry and interconnect wiring on the chip and hence the 16-bit microcomputers were introduced. With 16-bit words it became possible to make chips that controlled more complex applications, and more importantly, programmers could actually write programs more like those on larger computers.

A big break through came with the development of 32-bit word length chip computers. Finally the day had come where quite complex programs could be run similar to how previous generation mainframes could run. The longer the word length, the faster a machine could operate since runtime is a function on how fast data can be accessed in memory. Today 64-bit word length microcomputers are common place, only a dream back in the days of huge mainframes like the UNIVAC 1105. Back then it was considered impossible that one could compress the power of a supercomputer on a single chip.

A.4 Covering all my bases

At ARF/IITRI I was very familiar with using the octal number system on the mainframes I programmed. I thought in terms of octal, not hexadecimal. But when I was considering a job change, the new company I was going to join had ordered a IBM 360/model 30 that was not delivered yet. So I read up on the hexadecimal numbering system so I would be prepared for my job interview. I was introduced to the programmers I was to be working with. All of the programmers were programming in the COBOL programming language and would go to IBM headquarters in Chicago to run their programs on a 360 machine.

One of the programmers had a program error that he was pondering over. When an error occurred, the machine generated what is known as a memory dump that contained pages upon pages of hexadecimal numbers. He was stymied being an applications programmer and not familiar with such dumps. I inquired as to what his problem was and he said he couldn't make heads or tails of the dump. All he wanted to know was which line in his COBOL program contained the error.

I asked to see the memory dump and realized that it had a hexadecimal number pointing him to the error line in his program but one must do some arithmetic in hex to figure out where the error was. I wrote out the hexadecimal characters producing a long binary number of 0s and 1s. I then just broke it up in groups of 3 bits, i.e., essentially doing a hexadecimal to octal conversion, did the arithmetic in octal, then wrote out the result in binary and divided it into groups of 4 bits (binary to hexadecimal converversion) and from that showed him which line in his COBOL program was in error.

The person who was doing my job interview—and my future boss—was so impressed he hired me on the spot as a "systems programmer" to take care of, and program the new IBM 360 computer. Rightly or wrongly, I consider that little bit of "magic" to be responsible, in large part, for my new job.

Appendix B

Simplified election reports

This appendix explains in a little more detail the reporting of election results. Election reporting involves more than what first meets the eye. Looking at a newspaper after an election can look somewhat daunting with all the tables of listed election results. Although this appendix is not critical to the contents of this book, the material it contains gives additional insights into the process of election reporting using internet webpages with hyperlinks[1] to make the task more intuitive.

B.1 Election contests and ballot design

The general term applied to each item, whether an office or an issue, to be voted on is a *contest*. Contests are grouped in categories or levels as follows:

- *State-wide contests:* Some contests are national such as that of President which appear on all ballots within a state. Also included in this group are contests like Senator, Governor, Lt. Governor, Secretary of State, etc., that everyone votes on. These contests are included on all ballots.

  Following those are contests that are based on various districts defined within a state. The principle ones here are for U.S. Representatives where the districts usually cover more than one county.

---

[1] A hyperlink is that word or phrase that may be clicked on to go to a linking page. You might take a quick glance at Figure B.5 at the end of this appendix on page 163 that shows an overview of the linked reports to be discussed.

These belong to this state-wide category since they are national in nature.

- *County-wide contests:* These are contests like County Clerk, County Treasurer, county sales tax issues, and the like. Falling into this category are contests for various defined districts within a county that are not localized to a particular city, i.e., local.

- *Local contests:* These are local contests like mayors, city treasurer, city-specific issues, etc.

Looking at a ballot you will see that the ordering of contests usually follow in the order just mentioned. At the end of the ballot are generally placed the issues that require more room to explain each issue in greater detail. These too are usually placed in the order of whether they are state-wide or county-wide or local. Such an arrangement is generally adhered to by the ballot designers. The next time you vote, take a second to notice the contest arrangement. It is not arbitrary but follows a well-defined pattern.

Since each precinct may physically cover different districts—depending on how the districts are subdivided—a precinct may be required to have several ballots so the person next to you may have a different ballot than you have. All this gets somewhat complicated, to say the least, so the ballot design process requires some skill.

To ensure that ballots are properly designed, many locales employ outside services to create ballot designs for that locale. My employer, Election Resources Corporation (ERC), was primarily devoted to providing such resources to those who desire to take advantage of professionals who specialize in ballot design rather than do the process themselves. The final output of ERC was actual proofs of each ballot to be printed and the client would take these proofs to the printer of their choice to have the ballots printed.

ERC would, in many instances, confer with state or county officials and act as a consultant to local election commissions to avoid unnecessary problems. To get the ballot design wrong, especially if the ballots had already been printed, could become quite expensive. It should also be noted that different voting equipment also requires different types of ballots to be produced. The owner of ERC, had many years of experience in this sort of work and would frequently be interviewed on television as an expert during an election. Some of the ballots in Florida during the famous contested 2000 election were designed by ERC. In short, designing ballots is a rather complicated procedure with many potential pitfalls along the way.

During the 2000 General election, our client—the one I primarily worked with—was the Secretary of State (SOS) of one of the western mountain states (see Chapter 11). Their office inquired as to whether it would be possible to generate all the webpages they could put on the SOS's website. We said we could, and we did.

B.2 An example of a typical election

The best way to explain what the various reports that needed to be generated for placing on a website is with an example. Take, for example, a single state with two counties having two precincts each and two contests is about as simple as one can get.[2]

For our example, I'll call the two counties County A and County B. The two contests I'll likewise call Contest 1 and Contest 2. In a similar manner the two precincts in County A will be called Precinct A1 and Precinct A2, and likewise for County B, they would be Precinct B1 and Precinct B2. This arrangement is shown In Figure B.1.

B.2.1 Summary reports

The first category of reports that were needed are the summary reports on both the state, county, and precinct levels as shown in Figure B.2. Of course there would be only one webpage at the state level, that being the main webpage for the reporting website. For the summary reports on the county level we needed two reports, one for each county in our example.

---

[2]With our client, to produce reports for all the county-wide and local contests would produce far too many webpages, about 5,800 if my memory serves me correctly. The SOS decided that only the state-wide contests and those of national importance—such as those for U.S. Representatives—would be required. This amounted to some 480 computer files. To make it easier to upload these files—one for each webpage—I wrote a small program that would combine all these files into one large file every 30 minutes or so. I would then transmit that single file to the SOS's office where they used another short program I wrote to break them all apart so they could upload them to their website also described in Chapter 11.

STATE
    COUNTY A
        PRECINCT A1
            CONTEST 1
            CONTEST 2
        PRECINCT A2
            CONTEST 1
            CONTEST 2
    COUNTY B
        PRECINCT B1
            CONTEST 1
            CONTEST 2
        PRECINCT B2
            CONTEST 1
            CONTEST 2

Figure B.1: Report voting levels. The topmost level is the STATE itself for national and state-wide contests. The middle level is the COUNTY for county-wide and local contests. The lowest level is the PRECINCT, but note that there are no precinct level contests. Note also that districts like U.S. representative can span different counties and precincts thus there are no specific levels for districts. In our example we assume that these contests are state level so they appear on all levels. County-wide and local contests would show up at the county level but our client wasn't interested in showing those on their website.

In our example, we have a total of four precincts so the number of summary reports required would be four webpages. (In our client's state there were a couple of thousand precincts. The exact number escapes me. Some physical voting locations serve several precincts. They would report the total number of votes in a combined manner. Somehow the total number of 480 webpages sticks in my memory.)

The results are cumulative such that the precinct results are gathered together to form the county reporting results, and the county results are likewise gathered together to form the state results. These summary

Section: B.2

reports are of the same general format as shown in Figure B.2. They are presented in the contest order discussed in section B.1.

```
STATE Summary report
    CONTEST 1
            Contest 1 results
    CONTEST 2
            Contest 2 results
    etc.
```

```
COUNTY Summary report
    CONTEST 1
            Contest 1 results
    CONTEST 2
            Contest 2 results
    etc.
```

```
PRECINCT Summary report
    CONTEST 1
            Contest 1 results
    CONTEST 2
            Contest 2 results
    etc.
```

Figure B.2: Voting summary reports. There is only one state-wide summary report. For counties there will be one summary report for each county. And for the precincts there are as many summary reports as there are precincts. The number of precinct level summary reports would be quite large.

There will be only one webpage for the state-wide summary report. For county and precincts there will be one report for each county and precinct respectively. In our simplified example that means two county reports and four precinct reports since each county has two precincts. This makes a grand total of 7 reports that will be required. In an actual election this results in a large number of summary reports, i.e., webpages, needing to be generated.

The results are cumulative such that the precinct results are gathered together to form the county reporting results, and the county results are likewise gathered together to form the state results. These summary reports are of the same general format as shown in Figure B.2. They are presented in the contest order discussed in section B.1.

```
CONTEST 1
    COUNTY A
          Contest 1 results
    COUNTY B
          Contest 1 results
    etc.
```

```
CONTEST 2
    COUNTY A
          Contest 2 results
    COUNTY B
          Contest 2 results
    etc.
```

Figure B.3: County contest reports. The number of these reports is dependent on the number of counties in the election. Once again in our example there are only two contests.

B.2.2 Contest reports

Contest reports also needed to be generated as shown in Figures B.3 and B.4. Here the number of reports tends to grow greatly, not so much for counties but much more so for precincts since there are so many of them. For my task for our client, this is why it was decided to only generate webpages for the major national and state-wide contests. We had the data to produce all the contest reports but for county-wide and local contests the total number of webpages would grow into the thousands and our client was not interested in putting all that data on a state website.

B.3 Hyperlinking all the report webpages

When designing a webpage there are two ways to go about it. By far the easiest way is to design a static page which doesn't change over time. This is the way most webpages are designed on the websites one visits. A more sophisticated approach is to use a computer program to create webpages on the fly. At ERC we had quite a complex database that was continually updated during election day. The program I wrote would interrogate this database to literally build all the state's SOS webpages whenever the program ran. This meant that the logic used could tailor make all the hyperlinks any way we wanted. To tweak each hyperlink by hand, as is the case for static webpages, would be next to impossible with so much data being produced. I favor this latter approach, i.e., having a computer program do it, and have used it many times starting with the Toastmaster website I previously designed. The overall linkage scheme is shown in Figure B.5 but will be discussed in greater detail now.

```
CONTEST 1 for County A
    PRECINCT A1
        Contest 1 results
    PRECINCT A2
        Contest 1 results
    etc.
```

```
CONTEST 1 for County B
    PRECINCT B1
        Contest 1 results
    PRECINCT B2
        Contest 1 results
    etc.
```

```
CONTEST 2 for County A
    PRECINCT A1
        Contest 2 results
    PRECINCT A2
        Contest 2 results
    etc.
```

```
CONTEST 2 for County B
    PRECINCT B1
        Contest 2 results
    PRECINCT B2
        Contest 2 results
    etc.
```

Figure B.4: Precinct contest reports. The total number of reports at this level is generally quite large because it depends on the number of contests which would be large if county-wide and local contests were to be included.

Webpage navigation is always a problem with such a large number of webpages present. The best solution was to have only one webpage at the top, and this was the state summary report, i.e., the top report in Figure B.2. Each contest name had a hyperlink to the appropriate state level contest report as shown in Figure B.3. In that contest report one could click on the hyperlink for the county name. This in turn would take you to the webpage for the summary report—middle report in Figure B.2—that would show the summary results for that county.

If one was interested in going lower, a hyperlink was provided in the contest name that led to the precinct contest report as shown in Figure B.4. From there there was another hyperlink in the precinct name that led to the summary report for that precinct shown as the bottom report in Figure B.2 that showed all the results for the precinct.

All in all it was a pretty convoluted system of hyperlinks but easily navigated to find the data one was interested in. In other words, there were a number of different paths possible through all the webpages depending on what one was looking for. I also placed on each webpage some hyperlinks that allowed one quick access either to the previous webpage as well as to the state-wide webpage so they could start over again, say to a different county or precinct. Programming the computer to automatically generate all these hyperlinks as well as the webpages themselves was somewhat of a nightmare. Luckily, once done, all I needed to do was run the program and out came the complete set of webpages flawlessly as one big file.

Section: B.3   163

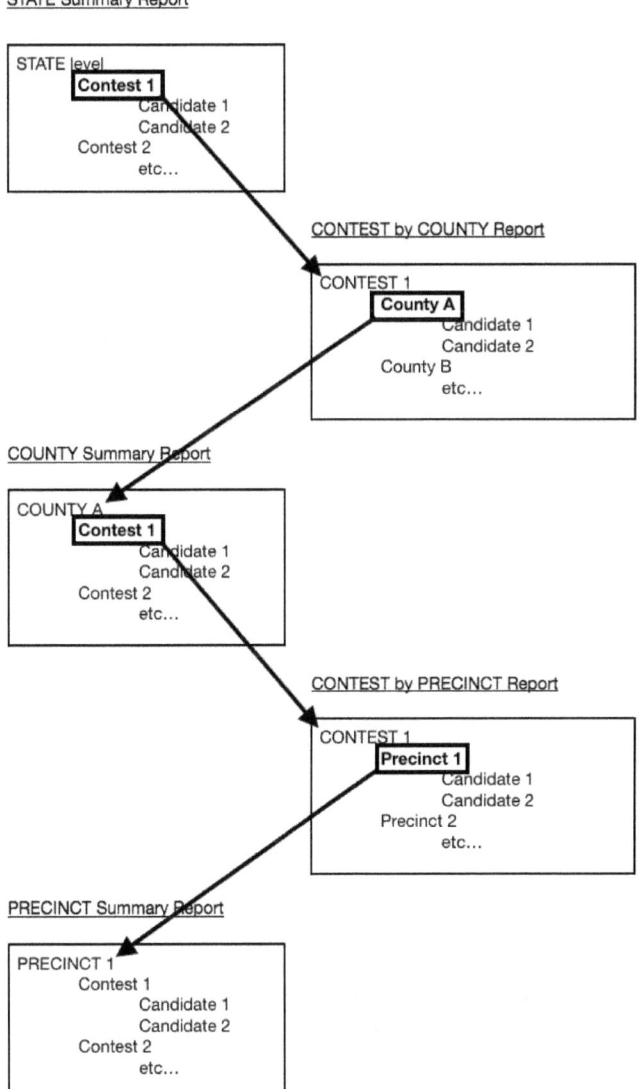

Figure B.5: Hyperlinking of result reports. The links are shown in rectangular boxes—only one link is shown for each report whereas each similar line would also have a link—with arrows indicating the linked page. In reality, hundreds of individual webpages were interlinked in this manner. Drilling deeper just involved clicking on individual links. The system was quite intuitive and easily mastered.

Appendix C

What is microprogramming

I debated long and hard about including an overview of microprogramming, but since this book is about my experiences with computers through the eyes of a systems programmer, I decided a brief discussion on this topic might be of interest. Skipping over it will certainly not detract from your understanding of the rest of the subject matter of the book. However, reading it will give you some insight into how many computers are designed today.

C.1 The problem

As computers grew in size and power, adding additional useful instructions meant adding new and more complex hardware. A typical example of this is testing bytes. It is easy to design a computer instruction to test a single byte but let's say a programmer wants to test a variable length string of bytes. This is akin to making a software routine which is easy enough to do in most programming languages but hard to do in hardware. The main drawback here is that a software routine might take considerable time. Wouldn't it be nice if there was a way to incorporate a time critical operation by being able to program it closer to the hardware level which would be considerably faster. By now you may have gathered how much I like speed.

Also another major problem is adapting an existing computer program to a newly introduced upgraded computer. It's very expensive to convert existing programs to run on a new machine. Just ask any company that was forced to do just that. Programmers aren't cheap!

In the early 1950s a man named Dr. M. V. Wilkes of Cambridge University in England proposed a new design philosophy for computers. His new design was to essentially make a computer within a computer. This is done by inserting a new layer between machine language instructions—the basic language that the computer understands—and the actual hardware itself (see Figure C.1). In this manner, if new hardware for faster operation was available in a new machine, that machine could be made to emulate an older machine without having to change any user programming for the older machine. This new layer would implement the ability to upgrade to newer and faster hardware easily thus saving any rewriting of existing software. The first major company to successfully design in this manner was IBM with its 360 and 370 series machines. A customer could start off with a less powerful computer, such as the 360 model 30, and later upgrade when more powerful hardware, such as the 360 model 50, was introduced. A customer could migrate with ease to the new hardware.

This new microprogram layer is programmed by the computer manufacturer, is implemented in hardware, and is transparent to even user programmers at all skill levels. In fact, most programmers don't even know such a layer even exists. This is called *microprogramming* and the program is usually stored in read-only memory so users can't change it. Later this concept was expanded by some manufacturers to replace a portion of the microprogram read-only memory with a small amount of RAM memory referred to as *control store*. This enabled a user-level systems programmer to essentially make new machine language instructions where time critical applications could take advantage of it. This was kinda neat at least in my opinion.

C.2 Computer timing

Every computer operates on a a basic clock. On early machines this was rather slow, usually being measured in fractions of a microsecond. On later machines this timing was much faster. This timing signal controls the execution time of each microprogrammed instruction. If, for example, a single machine language instruction was to fetch the memory contents from one location in memory and store that value in another memory location, that would require several microprogrammed instructions. Thus, one could exactly calculate how long that machine language instruction would take by simply adding up all the timing of the microprogrammed instructions needed to perform the operation. Today when you buy a new computer and the sales information states that the machine is a 2 GHz machine, this means that each microprogrammed instruction is executed in one half of a nanosecond or 2 billion microprogrammed instructions can run per second. Since it usually takes several such microprogrammed instructions to execute one machine language instruction, the execution time of each machine language instruction is much slower than the system clocking rate.[1]

Interdata took advantage of microprogramming in several interesting ways. One way was to use a different set of microprogrammed instructions to transform the 7/16 hardware into the 7/32. This was a fast, easy, and inexpensive way to turn a 16-bit machine into a 32-bit machine using the same hardware. The advantage of this was that 32-bit code could be developed on the 7/32 which was compatible with their anticipated newer product. Of course later they would introduce the 8/32 which was a true 32-bit machine, i.e., one with 32-bit data internal data paths rather than 16-bit ones.

Another way Interdata used microprogramming was to implement floating point arithmetic. One could buy a true floating point hardware board for a cost of several thousand dollars—about $5,000 plus if my memory serves me correctly—or move the logic to perform floating point operations into microprogram code. Of course the operations would be much slower than in hardware, but if little use was to be made of floating point, it saves a lot of money. Remember, I had mentioned elsewhere that anything that could be done in hardware could be done in software. After all, logic is logic no matter where it is implemented.

I never used microprogramming directly since I didn't have the need. However, I used the basic concept of it in the calculator I designed as discussed in Chapter 10 starting on page 121. I had the problem there of having to do arithmetic on long numbers for tax calculations. Since it was only a 8-bit microcomputer, I wrote some subroutines that performed those operations—especially multiplication and division—in the same

---

[1] An exception to this is what is called a Reduced Instruction Set Computer (RISC) where, by hardware design, each machine language instruction is executed in one clock cycle. Such machines are ideal for specialized applications where timing is critical but not very general purpose for many applications.

way that actual hardware would have done had it been available.

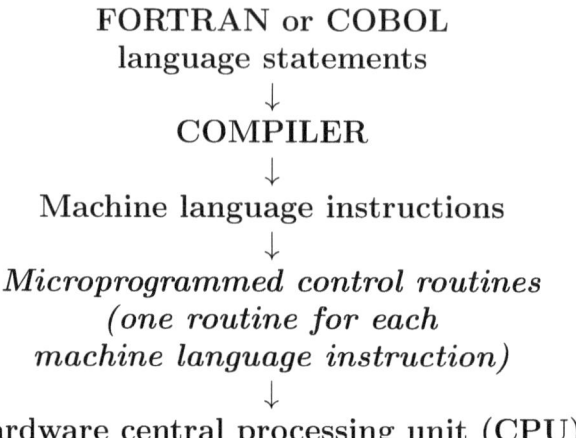

Figure C.1: Microprogramming level diagram. A higher level language like FORTRAN or COBOL runs their computer statements through a *'compiler'* to produce machine language output. (For an assembler program the program is run through an *'assembler'* which changes each line of coding to one machine language instruction.) For each machine language instruction there is a microprogrammed routine that controls the logic used to execute that instruction.

I hope this all too brief description of microprogramming will give you a better idea of how modern computers work. I personally thought this subject was quite interesting.

About this book

This book was written and typeset entirely on an Apple iPad in LaTeX (pronounced 'lay·tech' with the German 'ch' sound) using the iOS app called *texifier*.[2] I had previously used a LaTeX app on my iMac but decided to try the *texifier* app to see if I could accomplish all the specialized formatting functions like the iMac could. I was pleasantly surprised to find out it worked just as advertised.

LaTeX is a typesetting program originally developed by mathematician Professor Donald Knuth in the early 1980s to solve the problem of complex typesetting he was running into with publishing his own books. It seems that various publishers he tried could not get it correct with his manuscripts so he "rolled his own" program to do it properly. Since that time the popularity of LaTeX has grown worldwide. Various groups have been formed to extend the capabilities of the overall system such that today LaTeX is extremely versatile and comprehensive.

For anyone wanting to try this editing/typesetting program, I highly encourage doing so. But like with all programs with real power, there is an initial learning curve. To assist, there is excellent free documentation available that may be downloaded from the internet.

texifier has one nice feature that my iMac program doesn't have. It allows you to see both the text you type and the typeset result immediately displayed in a separate window. My kudos to the developers: they did a fantastic job with adapting LaTeX to iOS primarily for the iPad.

---

[2] The app is a text editor as well as a typesetter so it is all that's needed.

Index

1960 U.S. Census, 9

Acxiom Corporation, 115
AEC, 2, 24
AIC, 93
Allen, Paul, 143
AM versus FM transmission, 63
Amboy, Illinois, 39
Ampex tape recorder, 33
Analysts International Corp. (AIC), 85, 87
Anderson, Prof. Chuck, 141
Apple Pages, 19
ARF, 1, 153
ARF computer group, 6
Assembler, 168

Barcode, 108
Basic reference number (BRN), 50
Binary bit, 17
Blast shield design, 2
Boering, Brooke, 69, 77
Bonner, Ray, 60, 95
Bulletin board systems (BBS), 111
Bytes, 37

C programming language, 139
Calibration, equipment, 97
Camras, Marvin, 33
Cardiology conventions, 75
Carpet unroller, 106
Circuit board design, 97
COBOL language, 23, 46, 48, 89, 112, 133, 154, 168
Companies, other
    Apple corporation, 169
    Becton Dickinson, 103
    Boise Cascade Corp., 40, 57, 82
    Control Data Corp. (CDC), 79
    Healthtech (part of Telemed, 67
    Hewlett Packard, 108
    Hospital Corp. of America (HCA), 82
    IDM Corporation, 131
    Metromation, 59, 60, 67

    National Semiconductor Corp., 97
    Telemed Corp., 58–61, 67, 103
    United Airlines, 40
Compiler, 168
Computer architecture, 7
Computer companies
    Ampex, 33
    Control Data Corp. (CDC), 60, 90
    Cray, 56
    DEC, 59
    Friden, 11
    IBM, 5, 41
    Interdata, 60
    Sigma, 59
    Sperry Rand, 9
Computer data buses, 72
Computer data formats:
    Basic 2^n rule, 150
    Bits, 17, 149
    Bytes, 150, 152
    Nybble, 152
    Words, 152, 153
Computer data formats:Bases, 151
Computer timing, 6, 166, 167
Computerized ECG analysis, 61
Computers
    DEC Alpha, 115
    DEC PDP-11, 103, 104
    DEC PDPsystem10, 59, 82
    IBM 1401, 36
    IBM 1620, 25
    IBM 360, 152, 166
    IBM 360 models, 41, 166
    IBM 360 system, 37, 60, 96
    IBM 360/model 30, 40, 41
    IBM 370 series, 85, 88, 166
    IBM 650, 5, 6, 8
    IBM 7094, 28, 35, 36, 89, 152
    Interdata, 67
    Interdata 5/16, 143
    Interdata 7/16, 72, 167
    Interdata 7/32, 72, 90, 143, 167
    Interdata 8/32, 72, 94, 167

171

RISC, 167
Sigma 7, 59
UNIVAC 1105, 8, 9, 11, 88, 152, 153
UNIVAC 1108, 40
Zilog Z-8000, 107
ComputersInterdata, 143
Conway, Arkansas, 113

Dalhousie University in Halifax, 94
Dallas, Texas, 94
Data entry, excessive messages, 133
Database organization, 131
Debugging, remote, 102
Digital hardware logic, 96
Dillards Department Stores, 112
Disk drivers
    Diagnostic programs, 78
Disk drives
    10 MB variety, 78
    300 MB variety, 78, 91
    CDC variety, 79, 142
    Effects of magnets on, 79
    Error detection/correction, 79
    Flying heads, 91
Dixon activities
    Cancer Society, 56
    Elks club, 56
    Hardware design, 57
    Masons, 56
    Red Cross blood program, 56
    United Fund, 56
Dixon, Illinois, 39, 53, 54, 56, 74, 106
Dower, Dr. Gordon, 95
Drum storage, 7
Dvorak keyboard, 25

ECG analog data transmission, 99
ECG analysis programs, 95
ECG carts, 62, 142
ECG data transmission, 63, 64, 98
ECG pattern recognition, 95
ECG program timing, 95
ECG receiver, 65, 96
ECG Systems Corp., 93
ECG Systems Med-Call device, 98
Eichler Brothers, Inc., 39
Election contest reports, 160
Election contests, 155
Election summary reports, 157
Election, 2000 general, 130, 135, 136, 157
Elections Resources Corp., 129, 156
Electrocardiogram (ECG), 59, 62
Elgin, Illinois, 58, 60, 88

Field effect transistors (FET), 122
Fisher, Dr. David, 142
Floating point arithmetic, 167
FORTRAN, 23, 36, 59, 67, 94, 95, 168
Frequency generation, digital, 98
Friden Flexowriter, 11
Frist Sr., Dr. Thomas, 82

Gunn Systems, 105

Hacking on the UNIVAC, 20
Higher level languages, 23
Hoffman Estates, Illinois, 58, 59, 67
How the heart works, 61
Hyperlinks on a webpage, 135, 155, 160
Hypertext Markup Language, 132
Hypertext markup language (HTML), 118

IBM
    Cards, 11, 35
    DOS task scheduling, 68
    Drum storage unit, 7
    Field engineers, 43
    IBM 360 paper tape reader, 46
    IBM 360 peripherals, 43
    IBM 650 SOAP language, 23
    Keypunch models, 44
    Remote job entry (RJE), 89
    RPG language, 88
    Utility macros, 45
IBM 1311 disk drive, 42
IBM Bonner ECG program, 93
IBM card overpunching, 133
IIT, 1, 139, 141
IIT campus map, 2
IITRI, 1, 82, 153
Initial program load (IPL), 44, 47
Interdata microprogramming, 167
Interviewing technique, 68

Jauss, Prof. David, 140
Jensen, Prof. George, 141

Knuth, Prof. Donald, 169
Kroch's and Brentano's, 89

Labahn, Jim, 97
Land, Dr. Edwin, 34
Lawton, Ed, 57, 121
LCD display unit, 122–124
LED display unit, 108
Lieberman, Paul, 4
Little Rock, Arkansas, 68

MA in Interdisciplinary Studies (MAIS), 141
MA in liberal Studies (MALS, 141
Machine (Assembly) language, 45, 94
Machine language, 22, 67
Macro instructions, 43
Magnetic tape, 13, 94
Management style, 73
Masters thesis, 142
Maxlow, Dr. James, 143
Memory
    control store, 166
    Core, 18, 99–102
    eProm, 123
    RAM, 7, 123, 166
    read only, 166
Message digests, 137
Michael Reese Hospital, 88
Microcomputer versus microprocessor, 122
Micromanaging, 83
Microprogramming, 165, 166
Microsoft Word, 19
Minneapolis, Minnesota, 87
Multiprocessing/multitasking, 43, 73
Murry, Ed, 4, 38

NASA, 95
NBS, 137
NIST, 137

Op-code (operation code), 8
Op-code quiz, 88
Operating system power loss, 99
Operating system, my own, 99
Operating systems
    'Big Oz', 43, 45, 48
    IBM 360, 43
    IBM DOS, 43, 48
    IBM IBSYS, 35
    IBM OS, 43
    IBM OS/2, 112
    Interdata, 77
    Interdata 7/16, 77
    Interdata 7/32 and 8/32, 77
    Microsoft DOS, 100, 105
Oregon, Illinois, 53
Orlando, Florida, 84
Orwell, George, 41
Oscilloscope, 3

Paper tape, 11
Paper tape reader, 11
Pattern recognition in realtime, 99
Phase lock loops (PLL), 97
PL/1 programming language, 67

Polycarbonate, 108, 126
Porzel, Fran, 37, 38
Pretty Good Privacy (PGP), 111
Princeton, New Jersey, 59, 60, 66
Prober, 102
Program documentation, 134
Programmer classifications, 21

Rotary shaft encoder, 107

Schmidt trigger, 33, 34
Schmidt, Prof. Otto, 34
Seattle Living Computer Museum, 143
Seattle, Washington, 143
Secretary of state (SOS), 157
Secure hashing algorithms (SHA), 137
Shock tube data trace, 31
St. Vincent Hospital, 93
Sterling, Illinois, 55
Strong shock tube, 2
Suspense file, 49, 50, 102
SWIMM code, 27, 35, 40

Tax calculator, 121, 167
Teams, successful ones, 73
Teams, unsuccessful ones, 116
Telemed analysis program, 93
Telemed as a client, 90
Telemed corporate politics, 82
Telemed EPIC printer problem, 80
Telemed EPIC problem in Omaha, 90
Telemed EPIC system, 72, 91, 93, 142
Telemed MEPC printer problems, 80
Telemed MEPC system, 69, 70, 72, 142
Telemed MEPC system for HUP, 78
Telephone data transmission, 61
Toastmasters International, 117–119, 129, 131, 140
Transistors, 6

UALR, 139–141
UltraEdit, 131
Unit record equipment, 132
UNIVAC 1105, 139
    Air conditioning, 10
    Controls, 11
    Core memory stack, 18, 100, 102
    CRT display, 13
    Divided A/B drum, 19
    Experience with, 40
    Graphics program, 28, 29
    High speed printer, 14
    IT compiler language, 23
    Logic module, 16

Logic trace program, 27
Maintenance staff, 47
Operating system, 19
Operators console, 11
Paper tape reader, 46
Printer drum, 15
SWIMM code, 27
Tape control unit, 12, 46
USE assembly language, 23
Universal Resource Locator. (URL), 136
Usenet groups, 111

Vacuum tubes, 6
von Neumann, John, 7

Walnut Creek, California, 105
Webpage design, 131
Wilkes, Dr. M. V., 166
Wilson, Dr. Jim, 68–70, 91
Woodfield, Illinois, 87
Wyatt, Don, 104

Zimmerman, Phil, 111

www.ingramcontent.com/pod-product-compliance
Lightning Source LLC
Chambersburg PA
CBHW070637100426
42744CB00006B/716